How to Become a Dream Organization

Eight Things Leaders Need to Know to Promote Change and Innovation

What People Are Saying About

How to Become a Dream Organization

Insightful and practical, *How to Become a Dream Organization* offers actionable steps any change leader can, and should, put to immediate use. Oscar Amundsen effectively translates findings from years of academic research into an engaging guide that will help leaders avoid common change pitfalls.
Amy C. Edmondson, Professor of Leadership, Harvard Business School; Rank #1 Management Thinker of the World, by Thinkers50; author of *Right Kind of Wrong*

A must-read! Every leader will benefit from reading this practical roadmap on creating the kind of workplace which many can only dream about.
Dr Kirstin Ferguson AM, award-winning leadership expert; author of *Head & Heart: The Art of Modern Leadership*

Drawing from both strong research evidence and his own solid experience, Amundsen provides leaders with the kinds of advice they can really use — and that can inspire the best in those around them. A great resource for anyone interested in employee motivation and wellness.
Richard M. Ryan, Professor of Psychology at the Australian Catholic University, and Ewha University, South Korea; editor of *The Oxford Handbook of Self-Determination Theory*

This book is a wonderful tour de force in what a leader needs to know about enabling creativity and innovation in organizations. It is a thought-provoking book with lots of examples and it gives a clear understanding of the light and also dark sides of change processes. I loved the reading.
Lene Tanggaard, President of Design School Kolding, and Professor at Aalborg University, Denmark

This book is for anyone who has ever felt that things at work could be better, especially if they want to make a difference. Drawing on years of interaction with diverse companies and organizations, Professor Amundsen identifies eight themes which, in combination, lead to win-win outcomes for organizations and their employees. The discussion of each theme includes practical guidance and provides a solid grounding based in evidence for those seeking change.
Dr Peter Totterdill, Director, Workplace Innovation Europe CLG and Visiting Professor at Kingston University Business School, London

This compelling guide blends management research with real-world examples, making it a useful resource for leaders at all levels. It explains the fundamentals of a workplace culture based on extensive professional autonomy, as required for innovative and flexible organizations. With its clear and engaging writing style, Professor Oscar Amundsen manages to simplify complex concepts, making it easy to read and apply.
Louise Bringselius, Docent, and researcher at Stockholm School of Economics; elected as Leadership Speaker of the Year Sweden, by My Speaker

How to Become a Dream Organization

Eight Things Leaders Need to Know to Promote Change and Innovation

Oscar Amundsen

BUSINESS
BOOKS

London, UK
Washington, DC, USA

CollectiveInk

First published by Business Books, 2025
Business Books is an imprint of Collective Ink Ltd.,
Unit 11, Shepperton House, 89 Shepperton Road, London, N1 3DF
office@collectiveink.com
www.collectiveink.com
www.collectiveink.com/business-books

For distributor details and how to order please visit the 'Ordering' section on our website.

ISBN: 978 1 80341 817 9
978 1 80341 851 3 (ebook)
Library of Congress Control Number: 2024936172

A CIP catalogue record for this book is available from the British Library.

Design: Lapiz Digital Services

UK: Printed and bound by CPI Group (UK) Ltd, Croydon, CR0 4YY
Printed in North America by CPI GPS partners

Contents

To Monica, Sofie & Jakob

What good is it to gallop if you're going in the wrong direction?

Fridtjof Nansen, polar explorer

Preface

The detective Sherlock Holmes has a great admirer in his faithful friend, Dr Watson. But Watson is worried about his friend's persistent craving for cocaine. One day Watson screws up his courage and confronts him about his abuse. Holmes is not at all offended. He puts his fingertips together calmly before answering: *Give me complicated problems to solve; give me work. Only then can I dispense with my craving for artificial stimulants.* Fortunately, a complicated problem quickly turns up that needs solving.[1]

Things are not quite so dramatic for most of us. But the response from Sherlock Holmes makes an important point: We need something meaningful to occupy us, something that will challenge us. One of the most important sources of this is *work*. In contrast to Holmes, most of us work within the framework of an *organization*. Hence it is interesting to understand how organizations work. They can be large or small, and may be found in the public, voluntary, or private sector. Whatever the organization, they have a great impact on our lives.

There are also always special *reasons* that explain why organizations exist: They have all been established to perform specific tasks or realize particular goals. And there lies the second reason why it is useful to understand organizations: They are important for *accomplishing something*.

Fortunately, this book does not try to explain *everything* about organizations and leadership. That would have been a monumental task. My aim is rather to make a contribution within a defined area. My intention with the book is to illuminate *what strengthens the ability of organizations to change and innovate*.

In an unstable world this topic has gained in importance. Pandemics, polarization, galloping technological development, and demographic changes are all phenomena that must be dealt with – also on the organizational level. The ability to change and innovate is also unquestionably necessary if enterprises and society are to transform in a green direction in the time ahead.

Moreover, the realization that an enterprise must be *attractive* to its employees has taken an extra turn in recent years: The number of workers looking to switch jobs has increased. We were reminded of this trend in connection with the coronavirus pandemic. Many workers hesitated to return to their jobs after being laid off during lockdown.[2] The upside to all of this is that there are no conflicting interests here. It is indeed entirely possible to develop organizations that are good at change and innovation *while also* being good for their workers. As you make your way through the book, you will see that these two 'demands' are typically satisfied at the same time. It is both meaningful and attractive for most of us to be part of development.

When all is said and done, this book project is about you, the reader. My goal has been to develop and present research-based knowledge on this topic. But the main point is that *you* will find something that is relevant, interesting, and useful for you and your life, whether you are a leader, worker, consultant, or student. In this way, the book can contribute to improving organizations.

– Oscar Amundsen

PS to the reader: You will notice that there are some notes in the text. These can be found at the back of the book if you want to know which research sources I have used. There is no other information in the notes, so you won't miss anything by ignoring them.

One more thing: The book doesn't have to be read from start to finish to have meaning. Let us assume that you are curious about what the chapters 'Fearlessness' or 'Tolerance' have to say (see the Table of Contents). In that case, you can just jump straight to those pages.

Introduction

What is the point of this book?

How would you describe an ideal workplace? If you asked five random people on the street, they would probably give quite different answers. Of course it is hard for me to know what you considered to be important in your description. Nonetheless, some answers will have commonalities regardless of the person or type of workplace. This book will give you an answer using research on the ideal workplace. Then you can check to see what agrees with what you may have answered.

Let me clarify my position and stance right away: I am a professor in organizational research with a special interest in innovation and change. These are the 'professional lenses' through which I see the world in this book. This is the foundation for the description of an ideal workplace — or *organization*, as it is usually called in my field. More precisely, this book aims to answer the following questions:

> What characterizes organizations that are good at change and innovation? And are at the same time attractive workplaces?

I give the answer by outlining the ideal organization for accomplishing change and innovation, an organization that *at the same time* functions well for both leaders and employees. What does such an organization look like? What characterizes it — which are its typical features? This can be thought of as a kind of 'dream organization' (see the end of this chapter).

An organization is a powerful instrument for realizing goals. The specific goals for an organization can be formulated and reformulated according to changing circumstances. This book does not deal specifically with one goal or another. It is about *improving the instrument that organizations actually are* — an instrument to satisfy their goals.

The meaning of life

Do we really need a reason for attempting to improve something? Most farmers live and work in the age-old tradition summed up by the statement: 'The farm is going to be handed over to the next generation in better condition than when I took it over.' Improvement becomes meaningful in itself if this attitude is your backbone. For my part, I am employed by a university that is trying to offer meaning in its work through a slogan reflecting improvement: 'Knowledge for a better world.'[1] The academic field I am engaged in also has improvement as a fundamental element. The subject of organization has in fact been constructed around the word-triangle: understand — explain — improve.[2]

The psychologist Abraham Maslow put emphasis on our basic need for development and growth – but always *together* with the need for safety. In this way, life plays out as a dilemma between stability and change. Put differently, we want *both* stability *and* change, *both safety and development*.[3]

In a philosophical sense it is possible, however, to 'choose sides' in Maslow's dilemma. Some will find that what is most important is that our mind likes routine.[4] Others will claim that the potential for improvement is basically what makes it worthwhile to get out of bed in the morning. The idea that the world cannot be improved is therefore a world without meaning. Here is a philosopher who pointedly describes such a position:

> The meaning of life is to improve things. As long as there is room for improvement there is a point in carrying on the next mile. A meaningful life is accordingly a life that

> *tries* to improve things; a meaningless life is one that does not try.[5]

Perhaps this is somewhat hyperbolic and not everyone will fully agree. Nevertheless, it reminds us about one thing. Even if we may see ourselves as 'slaves of habit,' most will consider it meaningful per se to strive to improve our own work and the organization we belong to. In other words, improvement is an activity that has intrinsic value. This comes in addition to the fact that a better organization also makes it easier to realize other valuable aims and goals.

Change and innovation as the common thread

The question this book aims to answer is thus what characterizes organizations that are good at change and innovation, and that are attractive for the workers as well as the leaders. This has given me the following navigation points in my work:

The organization must first be able to *change* when necessary. Needless to say, there are many reasons why an organization changes. What distinguishes between the different types of change is what the underlying motive for the change is. Change can occur gradually and organically, not unlike a plant that grows and changes (slowly) of its own accord. Or perhaps it is simply circumstances that come into play. But the focus in this book is on *planned change*, that is, when someone in the organization has intentions to make changes in certain areas. It has been well documented that succeeding with a planned change is not an easy and straightforward matter.[6] But quite often it is necessary to bring about change, regardless of which sector we are taking about.

Second, the organization must have the ability to *innovate*. 'Innovation' has become quite a buzzword, and it is used in increasingly more contexts. It is obvious that the need for innovative thinking is rising in most industries and sectors. Today, innovation is therefore about more than technology, economy, and business. In this book, the concept of innovation relates to what happens when new ideas arise and are taken into use in a particular setting, thus creating a *break with the established ways* in the setting in question. 'What's new' may be big or small, and it may refer to new products, services, or ways of working. In other words, innovation always refers to a break with the way things have been done.[7] For most enterprises, it is advantageous to be able to develop something new for internal or external purposes. This applies in the private, public, and voluntary sectors.

It may go without saying, but without innovation we will never solve the major challenges we are facing. This applies to everything, ranging from pandemics and demographic waves to artificial intelligence and the green shift. Bearing all this in mind, innovation seems to be more or less an 'existential question' for the generation making its way into working life. Society needs organizations in all sectors that can break with (and develop) their own practice — and that can contribute to others breaking with their established practice and developing.

The organization described in this book must also be an attractive workplace. It is often said in speeches that people are a company's most important resource. This statement has evolved into a cliché, but that does not make it less true. It must always be added, of course, that people are always *more* than mere resources for an enterprise.

What does the dream organization look like?

The answer to the question the book poses may be outlined as an ideal organization — a 'dream organization'— characterized by the features shown in the diagram.

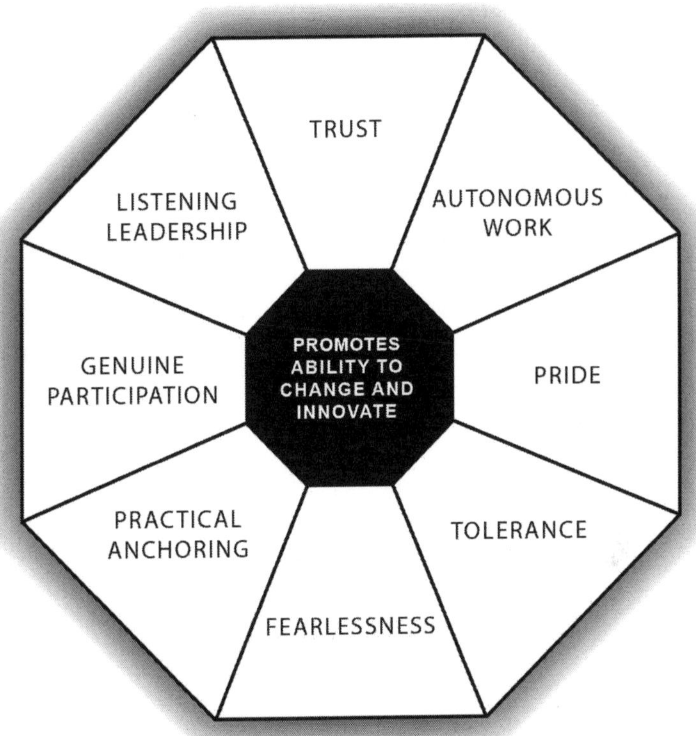

The Diamond Model for Change and Innovation

As you can see, there are eight messages in this model: All of them start with one of the eight 'outer' words and are then read through to what is written in the center. This will give you sentences such as: 'Trust promotes ability to change and innovate,' and so on. Each of these eight themes has its own chapter (reading in a clockwise direction from the top), thus providing the concepts in the diagram with content and reasoning. The idea is to show *why* and *how* these features have a positive impact on the ability of organizations to change and innovate.

The book also has a goal of a more practical nature: that you the reader will be able to contribute to making the organization you work in better — for yourself and for your enterprise. This is what is suggested in the book's subtitle, that the knowledge will be useful and usable for those who want to strengthen an organization through change and innovation.

The eight categories are relevant for all types of enterprise, regardless of sector or industry. The focus is on what is common and what unites rather than what separates. Two of the international icons in this field suggest that while there should be more thinking across sectors, it is somewhat uncommon:

> Many working within organizational studies have almost exclusively focused on either the private sector or the public sector or the voluntary sector, but not all three at the same time. We believe that this is an error ... All three sectors are increasingly intertwined.[8]

The goal of the book is, of course, to contribute to building your general knowledge about the topic. At the same time, it has been important for me to make it easy to use the insights to take concrete actions in your own workplace. This way, the book will become relevant in various settings. Some things will be easily recognizable and simple to transfer to your enterprise, while other parts will require questions such as: What does this really imply for me and my organization? What do we call this in our workplace, and what will this mean in practice for us?

Bad organizations: Should we talk more about the darkness?

I will use many specific examples to illuminate my points throughout the book. Each chapter also includes a special 'case narrative.' The aim of these is to provide insight into life in various types of organizations and situations. These eight narratives are not light and cheery. The descriptions are not of ideal states or 'best practice.' They are rather the opposite: a type of anti-narrative, more like a type of 'worst practice.'

There is no doubt that life in an organization can be dark. Consider for example how a person working in a storage facility in a big German city describes the situation:

> You're now standing in the meeting place by the shelves in the storage hall, with the cardboard box containing your work tools in your hands, and both feet planted right in the middle of the reality of life. Or perhaps you're immersed in the consequences of your financial situation and what the so-called labor market has to offer. A cold wind is blowing. You zip up your fleece under your reflex jacket and pull up the hood. One of the doors to the terminal does not close properly, and this is how it will continue, and later when you start to shiver you'll hear that there is no plan to get a space heater for your sake. You will say that you actually didn't ask for a heater. And then, when you really start shivering, you won't be able to repeat calmly what you really asked for (that the door should be fixed). You'll not just feel the chills that are coming up inside you, but those that have been there for quite some time already, and they are spreading throughout your whole body. Your time ahead will be full of misunderstandings. Just like always.

This quite grim story is from a novel.[9] The character appears to be maladjusted and alienated. The surroundings are cold, both physically and emotionally. We are very far from an ideal situation; indeed the contrast to an ideal situation is quite stark.

For many of us, a negative portrayal of working life will conflict with our own preferences. In her book *Bad Leadership*, the leadership researcher Barbara Kellermann writes that we have a natural tendency to focus on the positive, while choosing to eliminate the negative. This is because it is completely within our own interests to seek mental well-being. Therefore we prefer reading about the leadership of good leaders such as Nelson Mandela, rather than bad ones, such as Robert Mugabe. But her point is that it is difficult to see the light clearly without accepting that the dark also exists.[10] Because the dark is also there in working life.

Philosophy differentiates between two ways of experiencing the world. The positive experiences we gain on a continuous basis in everyday life confirm what we already knew. The negative experiences conversely have an utterly different potential for learning and new understanding. The trick is to see the constructive in the negative, as the authors of the book *Piss-Poor Leadership* claim. Their entire book is based on this point:

> It is through the negations that we seriously start to learn and experience things in a deeper sense.[11]

In spite of the idea that the dream organization is related to light and ideal conditions, darker contrasts are also explored in my book. Admittedly, though, not as dystopic as the report above from the storage facility. You will at any rate encounter realistic case-narratives from situations where things do *not* work that well. Such negations will contrast (and in this way illustrate) the various aspects of the dream organization. Thus, there is a possible negative version of the diamond model above. Here the features have been reversed so that they weaken the ability to change and innovate (see diagram).

The Reverse Diamond Model

There is no simple plus-minus relationship between the concepts in the model. This version of the model is not really important in itself (the previous model is the important one). The point is that it is necessary to talk about *both* what promotes *and* what inhibits the ability to change and innovate. It may not be obvious what is meant by all these concepts, neither the positive nor the negative. The answers will be found in the next eight chapters.

Chapter 1

Trust

Do you trust your colleagues? And does your leader trust you? In this chapter I will examine more closely the importance of trust in an organization. Let's start by listening to a successful top executive in the grocery industry. In his view, trust is the most important thing to learn for a person aiming to become a leader. Here is his reasoning:

> Too often progress comes to a halt due to lack of trust. Everyone has to be watched, everything must be noted. There is too much bureaucracy, and then it fails. We have to trust each other. When we can give and gain trust we can build an effective structure. Everyone has to get the point, that has to be your backbone.[1]

My aim here is not to analyze the above quote in any great detail, but some interesting points emerge from it. The first is that absence of trust means that control and follow-up are more difficult. Next, it is pointed out that trust is a two-way street; it is about trusting each other. This means that we are talking about *reciprocity* here.

The main message in this chapter is that organizations where there is trust between people will have an advantage when working on change and innovation. Therefore it is useful to find out more about the topic of trust. I will start with an example from everyday life in an organization:[2]

Freya's method

Freya is a 39-year-old healthcare worker in a nursing home in a medium-sized city. She has extensive experience in the nursing home's section for the oldest and weakest patients. As a committed and empathetic employee, Freya thinks a lot about her patients' well-being. One repetitive and labor-intensive job on an everyday basis is to change the bedclothes on the residents' beds. This is done regularly, and also every time something has been spilt on the bed, which happens quite frequently with this group of patients. The operation of changing bedclothes is quite complicated with these weak, elderly people, and several members of the staff must always be present, for example to operate the lifting devices. The time it takes to complete the process is also a significant burden on the patients because straps must be attached and tied in many places on their bodies when there is lifting to be done.

Sara, the section leader where Freya works, is known as 'firm, strict, and wanting things to be done by the book.' Sara has also made it clear that it is her duty to report all deviations in behavior and work in the section to her superiors.

On a busy afternoon when a patient spills milk on the bedsheet, and with no other co-workers around, Freya finds a new and untraditional way of changing the bedclothes. She goes to get a large rolled-up garbage sack from the kitchen (bigger than the regular ones you buy in shops). She carefully rolls it out under the patient. This makes it easy to (carefully) push the patient to one side of the bed, so she can remove the soiled bedsheet from one side of the bed and put on a new bedsheet on that side. Freya has the clear impression that the patient in question likes this change of bedclothes better than the traditional way based on lifting. The whole operation also takes only ten minutes, and she carries it out without assistance. Since this is a far more effective and probably qualitatively better way of doing this than the usual operation, one would now think that Freya would enthusiastically tell this to her co-workers in the section. However, exactly the opposite happens. Freya does what she can to avoid any knowledge of it being spread further by those who take over after her shift. This is done to keep section leader Sara from hearing about it. Freya assumes that her actions would trigger a reprimand and that she would also be reported upwards in the system for breaking the rules and procedures in the section.

It is not certain that Freya's method can be used on all patients. Also, it is possible that there are reasons why the method should not be used *at all*. The point in this context is that there appears to be a lack of trust between leadership and the employee(s) in this organization. Instead, there is an atmosphere of suspicion that seems to dominate both parties. Thus the nursing home (and the world at large) loses the *opportunity to assess and refine* Freya's method before it can be suggested as a new procedure. It has the potential to be an innovation which could be in the best interests of staff, patients, and greater society. It would also be far better for Freya if she could be open about this situation. It would simply make her job more attractive.

I will return to this story later in the chapter. First I will say something more precise about what trust is and, not least, what it does within an organization.

Trust is about reliability and risks

Many experts think that trust mainly relates to *expectations*, or more precisely, having positive expectations of others.[3] If you ask a person to keep an eye on your luggage for five minutes at a train station, you probably expect that the person will in fact do the job. In this case you are a *giver of trust*, and the person you ask is a *receiver of trust*. Before you ask, you will have made some type of assessment as to whether the person is reliable or not. But it *can* happen that the person doesn't care, and when you come back you discover they have left, and your luggage has vanished. There is no escaping the fact that trust also implies 'risk-taking.' This means that in principle a degree of uncertainty or risk is part of the deal, which then means that trust can be abused – with all the problems that follow from that. This point can be illustrated using the related expressions 'to believe something' and 'to have trust in something.' Believing that a new colleague will do a good job does not necessarily put you in a particularly vulnerable situation. It is only when you land in trouble (if your colleague fails) that the term 'trust' is relevant. One might say that trust as a concept loses its content when not linked to uncertainty and risk.[4] The question, therefore, is whether you would take the chance when something is actually on the line. Exactly this point emerges in the very definition of trust:

> Trust is the willingness to expose ourselves to risk in an area that is important to us, without knowing for sure whether the person we choose to trust will meet our expectations.[5]

It is the *reliability* of the trust receiver that determines the risk of misuse. The example from the train station where you place trust in a more or less random person does not deserve to be applied to life in an organization. It is not highly relevant whether you, the reader, would leave your luggage in the care of a stranger or not. However, I would conversely add the premise that trust receivers in your workplace generally *are* reliable. You can of course choose not to accept this principle. Nonetheless, this is the assumption when we want to examine what trust *does*, namely how it can be said to work in an organization.

How trust works in an organization

On a TV show called *This Is Norway*, the host states that the high degree of trust that Norwegians have in each other makes them richer because everything goes more smoothly in society. He illustrates his point by stating that only one external person is involved in buying a house in Norway (the real estate agent), while the same transaction involves all of six people in the US (according to him). We can see this as a valid point: Trust has the advantage that it produces lower transaction costs in society. But this book deals more specifically with workplaces and organizations. Therefore I will look into how trust works in organizations, in particular when it comes to work and collaboration.[6]

There is little doubt that there is better *flow of information and knowledge* in a situation with trust. This becomes obvious when there is absence of trust or direct mistrust. If you do not have trust in the person providing you with information, you will also more easily doubt the content of what is shared. Perhaps you would not send information to recipients you distrust. This is how information chains, even those that are very necessary, are ruptured, increasing the chance that more and more people will feel poorly informed. Under such conditions, where there is less knowledge-sharing, the ability to learn in an organization is also undermined. Above, we saw that Freya's distrust in her leader led to just such a result.

It will also generally be *easier to collaborate* when there is trust. The reason is simple: The road to the finished product or service carried out in an organization very often involves several persons. When you are working with something, it will therefore be reasonable (and often necessary) to build on work that others have done. The question is whether you trust the other or others who have performed the work, whom you now need to rely on in the further processing of it. Trust in this context means that you do not need to check (alternatively redo) what has already been done earlier in the work process. This is obviously a great advantage as it saves you time and effort. The story from the nursing home told us that *control* can become the reverse side of trust. I will return to this soon.

Actually, trust *increases the options the giver of trust has.* In the train station situation, you will be able to move about more freely when you do not need to drag your luggage with you — provided that you place your trust in a stranger. In a work situation, a leader who places trust in a co-worker in a particular field achieves a sense of *relief*. Let us say that the leader asks a new co-worker to keep an eye on a particular field of operations. This will allow the leader to focus on another field which may require more attention. In both these cases the person giving trust makes a risk assessment. In the case of the leader, who will have a long-term relationship with the new co-worker, it is really not necessary to show full trust or zero trust. It is possible for the leader to gain some experience of the co-worker, starting with small things. This means a *gradual* escalation of trust, with an accompanying escalation of risk. Anthropological research confirms this perspective by demonstrating that trust is not something that can be used up through use, but rather the opposite is the case: The more it is used, the bigger it can become.[7]

It should be added that *trust is simply less demanding in a psychological sense* than the opposite: It is mentally taxing on you to be constantly suspicious of the people around you, and over time it would wear most of us down. It is demanding to continuously take precautions when you are involved in the work others do. Anthropology points out that trust is a basic premise for social life. In practice, social participation simply assumes some degree of trust; thus, pure distrust is basically the same as pure madness.[8]

Trust is focused on the future

I have mentioned that trust is related to (positive) expectations, as this means that it has a future horizon. A very minor example can be found when driving in traffic, for example when you are at a junction in heavy traffic with no traffic lights where drivers are meant to merge in turns. You allow one car to enter on the assumption that the next driver will let you take your turn in a few seconds. If you cannot assume that you will be allowed to merge, such a scheme will not work. Transferring this situation to working life, we can say that trust is about 'relying on events that have not occurred yet.'[9] This way of thinking may be related to the topic of making changes. What if people do not trust what is going to happen in the time ahead?

To illustrate this, I will draw on a research project that pointed out that negative expectations could impede the process of introducing change.[10] In this case, poor experiences with previous change projects caused negative expectations to spread widely. The failed projects thus cast a dark 'future shadow' over the attempts to introduce change in the organization. Here is a report from an employee who does not see any reason to put trust in upcoming change projects:

> We have reached the saturation point when it comes to more and more new change projects. What you ask yourself first is what's left after the last one? We never see the effects measured. We just launch something new because it will be better. So that is the first impression, I think. 'Change project' might be a dangerous term because people then immediately start to roll their eyes.[11]

When the change work in an organization is already discredited, there is no doubt that it will be difficult to get people to commit to this type of process. In this case, the rolling of eyes is an obvious expression of distrust in the change work. The earlier change projects appear to have quite effectively left trust in ruins.

Trust and control

It is not controversial to claim that trust promotes innovation in an organization.[12] But it may be a point that is underestimated in some cases. The topic of control, which I promised to return to, is the perfect way to clarify things in this context.

In the story about Freya we saw that the organization's control system (exercised by the leader) undermined the organization's ability to innovate. The minor innovation the employee introduced here could have been brought up for discussion with all the workers so that it could possibly have been adopted and used or adjusted by co-workers. Fearing the leader and the control system, Freya wants to avoid this.

But it is a little too simple to postulate that control and trust are true opposites. In practice these two will exist in combination. Organizations do not have zero need for control over what is going on. The point is rather to be aware that there are links between the two, meaning that control measures can easily have an unfortunate effect on the organization. The introduction of a quality control system may be perceived as a sign of distrust in employees. Such a measure, introduced with good intentions, may thus become the start of a negative spiral of decreasing trust in the organization.[13] In general, there is reason to assume that increased control in an organization will detrimentally affect the internal motivation of the employees and therefore their creativity. Thus the 'impulse' to commit to innovation is undermined.[14]

The book *Pseudowork* points to the fact that in recent decades there has been a tendency to increasingly construct new control systems in working life. The authors strongly doubt that this has yielded better services in the public sector, or for that matter in the private sector. They are, conversely, quite certain of another effect:

> In only a few decades thousands of people have been given the work of registering, measuring, attending meetings and reporting. It is highly probable that we have paid a rather high price for our lack of trust in each other. Far too many hours have been used in the meaningless hamster wheel of pseudowork.[15]

Even if there is no either-or in the relationship between control and trust, there is good reason to be aware that a balance must be struck: What is the genuine need for control? Is there more control than necessary in this organization? Thus the heaviest burden of evidence should be on the control mechanism in a good organization. You should have good reasons for increasing control activities in an organization if innovation is important for the enterprise.[16]

Trust is a gold mine

Let me wrap up this chapter by summarizing the importance of trust for an organization. These are the four 'mechanisms' that explain why trust matters:

1. Trust increases the flow and sharing of knowledge and information. We tend to share information with people we trust rather than those we *don't* trust. This works both ways: We are less likely to accept information and knowledge from sources we don't trust.

2. Trust promotes workflow and collaboration. Here is why: If we trust a colleague's work, we can *proceed* based on what has been done. If we don't trust what people have done, we will go back to check and verify. 'Double work' is both inefficient and boring.
3. Trust provides relief for leaders. The reason is this: If you trust a colleague, they can 'take care of' tasks that you are responsible for. This *frees up* and strengthens your own capacity as a leader. Thus, it becomes easier to prioritize other important matters that require your attention.
4. Trust boosts mental capacity. The reason is that low trust creates psychological strain. Tired and suspicious individuals have little energy left. Thus, it's not easy to be creative and constructive.

Based on this, we can conclude that trust is a 'gold mine' for a business. However, there always comes some sort of risk with it — because you can never be 100 percent certain that things will turn out well when you trust someone. Therefore, it requires a certain kind of *courage* if you want to get access to this gold mine. This means that building trust within an organization starts with courageous leaders. When you, as a leader, demonstrate trust in an employee, the likelihood increases that the employee will reflect it back. In this way, you contribute to gradually developing a culture of trust within your organization.[17]

It should immediately be added that other factors will also influence employees' levels of trust in an organization. Research particularly highlights the experience of *fairness* as crucial for the development of trust among employees.[18] More specifically, this involves respectful treatment, fair procedures, and equitable distribution of resources. If you want to build trust, it is therefore important to consider how fair things appear to the average employee. One key aspect here will be to strive for as much openness and transparency within the organization as possible.

All in all, I hope that you now see what trusting relationships can mean for an enterprise. In an ideal world, there should in practice be trust between employees and between leaders and employees.[19] For leaders, this implies that they are willing to show trust. If it is to function, the offer of trust must also be accepted by the employees, and they must demonstrate trust in the leadership.

The main point of this chapter is that an organization that has trusting relationships will enjoy benefits when working on change and innovation. Trust is also attractive *in itself* for the leaders and co-workers in the enterprise.

Chapter 2

Autonomous Work

You are employed in your job to perform some work tasks. The tasks are more or less specified, but who really decides *how* you perform them? And if you are a leader: How much do you allow 'your' employees to have control over their own work?

In this chapter we will consider the importance of autonomous work. Research on innovation in fact suggests that there is a clear positive relationship between autonomy and innovativeness in an organization.[1] Why is this so? This is the question we will examine in this chapter.

First, let us have a look at someone who has gained personal experience in this field. Here is a little story from the CEO of an energy company:

> When I started here, a somewhat clearer management-by-objectives approach was required. Therefore, from the start I made it clear that 'here we have to satisfy such and such goals,' you know. So you know what happened? The organization became a bit more passive ... it seemed that people started thinking 'OK, so now things are done from the top' ... So what we're working with now is to strike a balance between autonomy and control, you see. We have many incredibly talented people here, and they must – within the framework of our strategic direction – be allowed to find the way themselves. So now we're adjusting, bearing exactly this in mind: Where is the right balance between control and autonomy?[2]

Something happened when this CEO took steps to be clearer. We find her being surprised that her steps triggered a kind of passivity in the organization, which she (of course) saw as a problem. She is now looking for the solution in the balance between control and autonomy. Here the term *autonomy* is used instead of its synonym, 'self-governance'— and it is explained as 'finding the way yourself.'

If the employees are to 'find the way themselves,' *the leader's role* will also move away from traditional ideas of leadership. We shall start with a specific example to illustrate the point:[3]

A frustrated leader

Thomas is 46 years old and working as a leader of a medium-sized IT company in the capital. Most of the employees are engineers working with coding, and the company is doing well financially. Thomas is an ambitious leader who wants to be a model for the others and contribute by 'performing active and good leadership' over his employees. He calls it leadership with a capital L.

The problem, according to Thomas, is just that the employees do not appear to have any wish to be led. They are not very interested, neither in him as a leader nor for that matter in what he has learned through several leader-development courses about various forms of leadership (transformation leadership, coaching leadership, and so on). This is not what Thomas envisioned his leadership would be like, and he is a bit frustrated and worried. When two researchers contact him to study his company, he initially hesitates, but then thinks that it could even be fun to obtain a view from an external source. It is also completely free, apart from the time spent when the researchers interview the personnel.

The study by the researchers shows that the employees are more or less satisfied with their leader. But it also confirms Thomas's fears when it comes to his interest in exercising leadership of the company. When asked about his leadership the employees say things like, 'Oh well, it's good that he makes budgets and administrates the company ... We go to his meetings and answer his questions, but beyond that, what else is there to say, really?' When asked what a leader should do in his organization, the following response is heard: 'It should be somebody who arranges ... entertainment, parties and the like.' This in fact agreed with the practice Thomas had already developed, where, for example, every morning at five minutes to nine, right on the button, he would walk along the corridors announcing that 'breakfast is served.' He had the clear impression that this was appreciated, so he wanted to continue this. Thomas would also be arranging a beer-tasting event before Christmas and had booked a boat trip for the workers in the summer. He had heard that this too had been praised by the employees. But this role did not agree with Thomas's idea of what exercising leadership meant, hence his frustration.

If we disregard this leader's administrative and entertainment activities, the employees are not very interested in his leadership. They do not at all consider themselves 'followers' who need to be 'led,' transformed, or coached. Rather they see themselves as highly competent and clearly among the elite in the industry. The leader acknowledges that it is difficult to 'lead' since he does not understand what his employees exactly do in their work. The software development the company is doing is highly specialized and sophisticated. Most of the time, the employees sit facing the PC, writing programming code. They work independently, usually alone, and they do not always offer their leader insight into what they are spending their time doing. The conclusion reached by the researchers thus states: 'This leader dreams of leading his staff, but the demand for this is low. The engineers working for him want autonomy, not leadership.'[4]

Thomas's story makes it interesting to look into a book with the revealing title *Tempt Me Not into Leadership*.[5] The author of the book, who has been a leader, is blatantly honest about his experiences. His reflection is that he wanted to be a leader for the wrong reasons. The author says that his personal ambitions were the impulse behind wanting to be a leader, but that he immediately discovered he did not like it. For example, he was 'disturbed' by employees who wanted to discuss quite mundane matters, such as the content of the fruit basket (more kiwis, please!) and the wrong temperature in the offices. This is his summary of why he was not fit for the role of leader: 'You must have a genuine wish to ... lift others. And perhaps even be the leader who is *not* standing at the front, but the leader standing in the back. That was difficult for me.'[6]

The above examples may appear somewhat caricatured or exaggerated in our context. There is no reason to move from a ditch with *too* strong leader orientation to another ditch where we underestimate the importance of leaders.[7] So, we cannot at all conclude that the leadership role, in general, is unimportant — even if employees do not always request the form of management the leader wants to exercise. Leadership duties must continue to be addressed when it comes to strategy, administration, budgets, conflict solving, and hiring — just to mention *a few* (for now). But the point so far has been to remind ourselves about the importance of employees controlling their own work, and that this often results in organizations doing well. The impulse or *motivation* of the employees in the examples above is found in the performance of their own work. We will therefore look more closely at the topic of motivation. This a keyword in this chapter.

There are several types of motivation

While the most famous pop music duo is Lennon & McCartney, in motivation research Deci & Ryan are the reigning duo, due to their theory of human *self-determination*. The theory, developed in the 1980s, has since been thoroughly tested and studied through several decades of international research.[8] To obtain knowledge about the topic of self-determination and motivation it is necessary to examine this research more closely.

The point of departure for the theory is that we are born curious and have the power to act. We are furnished with the will to learn and use our knowledge in reasonable ways. If you have spent time with a 5-year-old you will recognize this energy — which we can also call *motivation*. However, the drive and energy to learn may be undermined, and at times even disappear. When you were young you will probably have been in the same classroom as one or more non-motivated pupils (and you may have been one of them yourself at times).

Research in this field shows how the social environment around a person affects motivation. Not least, researchers are interested in what strengthens and what undermines motivation. To give a good answer to this, it is necessary to distinguish between *different types of motivation*. We would quickly get bogged down in this field if we were to only talk about strong or weak motivation. It is thus *type* of motivation, not just quantity, that is the key to understanding how this works.[9] Let me start on the next stage by asking you: What do *you* think people in general are motivated by in their job?

Are you thinking X or Y?

As a lecturer in the subject of organizations, I sometimes notice that discussions come to a stop in a particular way. The students have typically split into two opposite poles, and from there they cannot move on. The reason often boils down to two hidden assumptions about what really *motivates* employees in an organization. These two poles can be described thus:

> **X**: I assume that most people would rather do as little as possible. But I believe they can be encouraged to contribute by means of the 'carrot and the stick.'
> **Y**: I assume that most people want to learn and develop. And they want to contribute to the organization to satisfy its goals.

These two positions can be recognized in what is called 'theory X and Y,' developed by the renowned leadership researcher Douglas McGregor in the 1950s.[10] Let us examine the reason that the discussion stops at these two assumptions: *The organization* appears very different for a person believing in theory X than for a person who believes in theory Y. Hence, leadership efforts and any measures adopted become very different. The adherent of X becomes very engaged in checking that people are actually doing their job and may set up smart reward systems to ensure this. A person thinking Y will become more like a *facilitator* for the employees.

Those who build on theory X may well roll their eyes over such a 'soft' description of the leader, even calling it a naive 'curling leadership.'[11] Others will nod, recognizing that much of the leader's role means being a facilitator for others.

Intrinsic or extrinsic motivation?

It is because of the discussion above that the distinction between intrinsic ('internal') and extrinsic ('external') motivation enters the picture.[12] The question is where the *main source* of motivation comes from when you work: Are you only in it for the money or does the job provide any meaning in itself? The two types of motivation can be described thus:

Extrinsic motivation: Your motivation comes from what is beyond the work description. The work you do is mostly a means of being paid, getting praised by the boss, or possibly being promoted to a better job. External motivation may also be about avoiding trouble or punishment, or not losing your job.

Intrinsic motivation: Here motivation comes from carrying out the work task *in itself*. You do the job because it pleases you, gives you joy, or is experienced as meaningful in other ways. Your own wishes to do what is 'right for the company' may also be counted as a form of intrinsic motivation. We will deal with this in the next chapter.

In practice we will of course act according to a mix of intrinsic and extrinsic motivation. We might work to earn money, yet most of us would carry on doing our job even if we won a large lottery prize.[13] In other words, our pay is not the *only* reason that we get out of bed to go to work. In the same way, we might like a work task in itself, while we *also* think it is good that we are paid to do it. The situation will also mean something: In our daily work the intrinsic motivation may drive us, but extrinsic motivation may become more dominating in certain situations. An example is when you need to 'choose a direction' (should I join that project?), or when you are negotiating your pay.[14]

Motivation researchers have given these issues much attention.[15] They claim that it will be difficult to understand what goes on in an organization if we believe that reward and punishment are the main motivators for most people (what we called 'extrinsic motivation' above). Therefore they are critical of those who primarily believe in theory X. They believe that many leaders similarly overestimate the need for control and external reward. If we ask workers, research shows that intrinsic motivation is more important as a motivating force than extrinsic motivation. Therefore much time and energy are wasted on control measures, a management-by-objectives approach, and reporting — perhaps particularly in public enterprises. In the previous chapter we saw that such measures may easily be understood as signals of a lack of trust in the person or persons the measures are directed at.

How can we then explain the tendency to overrate external motives at the expense of internal ones? In an interview on this issue, one of the motivation researchers makes an interesting reflection on how an 'incorrect connection' can be made between the internal and external. A leader has access to his or her *personal* intrinsic motivations but does not know what is going on inside other people's minds.[16] Thus it may be easy to interpret the actions or behavior of others as being governed by extrinsic motivation ('I believe what I see'). As a leader, then, there is a reason to ask oneself: Why would *others* have less intrinsic motivation than I have?

In research on reward systems, another interesting matter has come to light: the so-called 'undermining effect.' This point can be illustrated by the story of the IT company and its leader, Thomas. Here our point of departure is the job of one of the employees in the company. Astrid is an engineer with a demanding work task that she finds interesting and meaningful in itself. Thus we can say that she is internally motivated for the task. Thomas, Astrid's leader, understands that her job is demanding. He also sees that she manages her tasks well. He believes that it is very important for the company that the task continues to be performed with good quality. Thomas now asks himself if he should introduce a system with financial reward for performing this difficult task. Earlier we saw that Thomas has a strong (but perhaps unexpressed) wish to contribute 'more leadership' in his role. What should he do?

The conclusion must be to tread carefully: There is reason to doubt that he will achieve the desired effect; it could in fact be the opposite. The introduction of a reward system may be like waving a shiny medal in front of an employee who, regardless, is moving steadily forward under her own power. A greater review of research in this field shows that a stronger focus on external rewards will reduce the intrinsic motivation for performing the work task.[17] Such a new system may thus undermine the company in the long term.

Freedom and control

It is appropriate here to be reminded that people are driven by *more* than reward or punishment. The distinction between extrinsic and intrinsic motivation is useful, but not enough in our context. To connect the topic of motivation more closely to autonomy we must return to Deci & Ryan and the theory of self-determination. For them, the most important dividing line is not between intrinsic and extrinsic motivation.[18] They are more interested in how 'free' or 'controlled' you feel when you act. As an illustration consider two situations:

A. *Controlled*: Here you experience being 'pressured' in certain directions when you act. You act according to this pressure, which may stem from external or internal 'sources.' An example of external pressure may be the need for money, while internal pressure may come from a need to avoid personal shame or a sense of guilt.

B. *Autonomous*: Here you experience that you can choose freely what you actually want to do. You act according to something inside you, and in agreement with your will. Here you may be purely internally motivated for the task; that is, you are driven by desire and interest. But there may also be external motives: You choose to do things you know are important and right for the organization but which also *agree* with your own goals and values.

We see that situations A and B will be experienced quite differently. It is precisely this sense of autonomy, namely how much you control your own choices, that distinguishes between the two. In the former, self-determination feels low, while it feels high in the latter. In the practical world there are obviously situations where you do not feel either completely in control or entirely self-determined. In professional literature, the term *autonomous motivation* is used for the way things play out in situation B.

Many studies show the benefits of facilitating autonomous motivation in an organization.[19] The effects are positive not only when it comes to effort and performance, but also for how well you are doing at work. The autonomous motivation theory attaches equal importance to both 'sides' of the matter: Performance and well-being go hand in hand. We can also note that research findings show that autonomy increases creativity and increases knowledge-sharing with co-workers.[20] Both are good for promoting innovation in an organization: Creativity is a raw material required to achieve something new. We must also recognize that innovation is rarely a solo achievement; it is rather a collective performance.[21] Hence, knowledge-sharing and information flow in the organization are important.

In change activities it will also be advantageous to understand the importance of self-determination. This means that change processes should be organized so that employees have influence on what may affect their work. This is not to say that everything, including every minute detail, must be subjected to discussion in the change process. But it does mean that leaders should not pursue their changes so eagerly that they may undermine the motivation of the employees — the fire within. The source of much of the motivation is precisely this sense of autonomy. In practice this means that leaders must *listen* to the input from employees in the change process, and that the employee participation must be *genuine*. Some might argue that this advice is bordering on the banal, moreover that it is more easily said than done. The answer to that is that 'genuine participation' and 'listening leadership' are two topics that have been given their own chapters later in the book.

A self-determined employee

The need for self-determination is defined as a basic human need by Deci & Ryan. This implies that employees in an organization will *actively* seek and choose situations that can satisfy this need. Indirectly this becomes the 'true' explanation when it comes to why self-determined work is important for an organization: We are motivated and thrive when we have a certain autonomy or *authority* to determine how we carry out the work. But Deci & Ryan are realists. They are fully aware that work motivation will always be a mix of various types of motives (we also work for money). Their point is that *autonomy is a necessary and essential part of the mix* if you want engaged and well-functioning employees in an organization.

Deci & Ryan's conclusion agrees with this: They assert that most workers actually *want* to contribute, experience mastering their skills, and feel they are a meaningful part of an organization. There is little doubt that they place themselves closer to theory Y than theory X, which we suggested earlier in the chapter. They also realize that there is a good deal of the carrot-and-stick approach, theory X, in many workplaces. One reason for this is that strategies based on theory X can become a 'self-fulfilling prophecy.' For an organization this may become a vicious circle. Leaders under pressure may be tempted to rely on the carrot-and-stick approach. Introducing such systems might actually result in increased productivity. But the effect is short-term and the system will therefore have to be intensified. For their part, employees will increasingly focus on the system, which in turn confirms the thinking of the leader about how important it is, and then on and on. In this vicious circle the feeling of self-determination and hence vital sources of motivation disappear into thin air.

In practice this means that leaders must be willing to give their employees certain liberties to test out new things and decide things themselves. For lack of a better term we can call this 'leadership supporting self-determination.'[22] The point is that you, as leader, delegate a degree of responsibility and authority to individuals (or a group) — *even if* you still have the ultimate responsibility. We see that the question of trust quickly surfaces here. In the previous chapter we saw that trust is having positive expectations about people, but it also means 'taking a chance when something is at stake.' The conclusion is therefore to take a chance on self-determination.

Chapter 3

Pride

Are you proud of the job you are doing? Are you proud of your workplace? In this chapter we will examine more closely the importance of pride in organizations. In my opinion this topic has not been given the attention it deserves, which may be because the importance of feelings has *generally* been under-assessed in organization studies.[1] Another reason may be that the word 'pride' is perhaps somewhat ambiguous. When the dictionary says it is used about a person who has self-esteem and is triumphant and confident, it can easily be associated with negative features, such as arrogance and exaggerated faith in one's own skills.[2] This chapter works with a far more positive meaning of the word. For example, here, when an employee in the social health service talks about his job:

> I'm proud to be working in the social health service. You probably think I'm out of my mind saying this because you only read negative things about us in the newspapers. But I'm proud of what I do. In fact, I've been given the valuable task of helping those who want my help.[3]

This, it must be said, is an entirely positive feeling, even though the individual telling the story is familiar with the media's critical view of his workplace. The next example shows that pride can also be attached to being part of a community. Here a grocery store employee talks about his job:

> It's like playing on the national football team. When you first put on your uniform you're fit for the fight, whether it's a price war or whatever.[4]

Here too we see positive feelings for the workplace, with a sports-team metaphor. Commonly, when a nation's football players are interviewed, they will express their pride in playing 'with the flag on their chest.' The quotations above touch on topics we will examine later in the chapter: the meaning of the job, bonds to one's own organization, and the importance of positive feelings. But first, a little about why I choose to write about pride.

A short story about research

Even though the word has a degree of ambiguity, 'pride' has been chosen as one component in the description of the dream organization. The reason for this is the following: Some years ago I joined a research project dealing with the role of employees in innovative work.[5] We wanted to examine this by studying organizations that 'had got this to work.' That means they had succeeded in engaging their employees in development and innovation in their workplace. Bearing this in mind, we visited various types of business to talk with people there about innovation. Our sample base was large, ranging from geriatric care institutions to IT companies and government departments.

Naturally, this work has left its footprints in this book. More specifically for me, there is one special aspect I recall from this project. First I remember the very open and welcoming way we were met by so many. That is not a given for a researcher. Not everyone has such a relaxed attitude to a visit from us. Some people become a little unsettled and go silent when strangers come to pry into their secrets. In this project, however, completely different feelings dominated. People were almost falling over themselves to show, tell, and explain. There was an underlying (but strong) sense of *pride* among the people we talked to. Here is an example of how pride surfaced when employees talked to us:

> You must include that the well-being factor is high; people enjoy being here. Only a few switch, quit, or go for other reasons ... I attended a meeting recently, and they were talking about people who had been hired as temps from another company. They said it was so nice here that they would like to come back. That it was so easy to establish contact with people here, and I really think that is something to bear in mind.

The working environment creates a sense of pride here, and the employees are hinting that you would be happy if you could get a job here working with 'us.' This expresses the sense of *belonging* that this employee has. I will return to this topic.

An employee in another company talks about how they have a bit of a reputation:

> We certainly have a reputation. I can honestly say that we are a place for development. We are known for not only having good ideas but also for managing to implement them. And I really believe that we have established a good reputation for that. We're considered a partner it is useful to collaborate with, that's for sure.

Here too we see the positive feelings generated by their own organization. It is both attractive and meaningful to belong to a 'we' such as this. This eventually became clear to us as we worked on the research project. This form of pride was a common characteristic of the various organizations we visited.

Traditionally, psychology has mostly focused on negative feelings at work (such as stress and conflicts), and the importance of these. In recent years psychologists have developed more interest in the importance of positive feelings at work. Now we find studies showing how positive 'moods' can promote creativity and innovation.[6] The pattern of positivity and pride we found across the organizations we visited was not something that existed by chance. I will return to this later. First we will look into a somewhat darker side of the issue.

Meaningless work

We have now heard from employees who directly or indirectly express their pride in their workplace. It is clear that their work gives them meaning in the form of well-being, recognition, or special tasks. The need for meaning is fundamentally human, and work is obviously an important source of meaning for many of us. As a rule we will be unhappy if the work we do seems to be completely meaningless. The famous author Fyodor Dostoevsky touched on this theme in one of his books. Here he writes about work with no meaning where the character is in prison:

> Even if the forced labour is uninteresting and dull, it has in a way a reasonable purpose. The prisoner makes bricks, digs in the earth, casts and builds. This work has meaning and a goal. But if he was forced to pour water back and forth between two buckets or move a pile of dirt from one place to another and back again, I think he would hang himself within a few days. Just to escape the shame, degradation and pain.[7]

The point is presented in a dramatic way, but the message is clear: Meaningless work is a very hard grind. And there is work without meaning in today's working life. Here an employee, Becky, talks about her job as a 'welfare coordinator' in a geriatric center:[8]

The meaningless form

Most of my work consisted of interviewing residents and filling in what we call a recreation form to identify the resident's preferences. After completing the form it was registered and logged on a computer, but then immediately forgotten forever. The paper version of the form was also for some reason archived in a folder. My immediate superior considered that filling in these forms was by far the most important part of my job. He hassled me very much if I was slow in logging the forms. Much of the time was spent interviewing short-term residents who moved away the next day. I threw away mountains of paper forms. The interviews were generally only a nuisance for the residents because they realized this was meaningless and unnecessary paperwork. And that nobody really cared about their personal wishes for entertainment and activities. I spent much more time identifying the activities residents would like than on starting any activities for them. Fortunately I managed to play piano for them every day before dinner, and then there was laughter and a good mood. These were nice interludes, but the main job was the forms.

This type of work is called a 'box-ticking job.' The focus in such jobs is on 'ticking off' that certain things have been done (here resident interviews) – but *independently* of whether what you are doing is contributing to what the organization is supposed to be doing. In the case above, not only is the biggest task meaningless but it also gets in the way of work that *could* have given meaning (to entertain and activate the elderly). Under such conditions it is not easy to be a proud employee, something this story illustrates all too clearly.

The point, more precisely, is that Becky wants to *matter* to the residents. When she plays the piano for them, she adds value to others, and she feels appreciated for her contribution. In a research context, this situation is known by the term 'mattering.'[9] The concept refers to a basic human need to find a good balance between feeling valued ourselves *and* adding value to others. Mattering leads to increased well-being for people, through a sense of self-worth and real purpose.[10]

The problem for Becky is that most of the work in the geriatric center feels meaningless. Consequently, it becomes difficult for her to thrive. We also learned that she eventually chose to leave this job. This leads to the question: What different reasons do we really have for staying in our job?

What creates bonds to an organization?

Some research has looked into what is called 'commitment' to organizations. This concept is used with different meanings in everyday language, while in academic contexts it addresses what we call 'organizational commitment.' Furthermore, we will apply a somewhat more restricted understanding by talking about what creates bonds or a sense of 'belonging' to an organization.

Organizational commitment refers to such issues as:[11]

- Do you believe in the organization's goals and values?
- Are you willing to make a substantial effort on behalf of the organization?
- Do you have a clear wish to maintain membership in the organization?

The first bullet point refers to how much you identify with the organization's *purpose*. The British author (and YouTube star) Simon Sinek has made a living out of talking about 'finding your purpose' for organizations that want to succeed.[12] One of his points is that it is necessary to attract and keep hold of young employees. From an academic stance, the importance of 'purpose' is no doubt a relevant point.[13] As we saw initially in the chapter, you can be proud of your workplace simply because it has a good working environment. But we also saw that pride may be related to the overarching purpose of the organization.

Organizational commitment also refers to how *involved* you feel. For someone who is deeply involved, what happens with the organization will be personal. An employee with strong ties to an organization will be keenly aware of its needs and will be interested in how to contribute to satisfying these needs. As the third bullet point shows, commitment implies that one wants to hold on to the job — even if there are other attractive alternatives.

According to the best-known model in this research field, we have three types of bonding with an organization:[14]

1. First there is an *emotional* commitment to the organization. This refers to the positive emotions one has from being part of the organization. Strong emotional commitment is engendered because you agree with the goal and values of the organization. This is the commitment Sinek has addressed with his message about 'purpose.'
2. There is also what is called a *normative* commitment. This deals with your perceived commitment to continue in an organization. The model implies that you experience a type of pressure from others in the organization to remain there, and that you are also worried about the reactions of others if you quit.
3. The third type is a *rational* commitment. This is more about rational cost-utility assessments of whether to

> continue to belong to the organization. The point is that you want to carry on because it would cost too much to leave. These costs might be related to financial concerns and your wage, but also to losing contact with co-workers and the camaraderie at work.

The researchers behind the model point out that employees can have varying degrees of all these bonds, and the three may function independently of each other. You may for example have a strong rational commitment due to good pay and good colleagues while caring little about the purpose of the organization.

All three types of bonding have in common that they bind employees psychologically. The stronger the bonds, the less probable it is that you are thinking about leaving the organization (or that you actually do so). The model can be summed up thus: Employees with strong emotional commitment remain because they want to, those with strong rational commitment because they must, and those with strong normative commitment because they think they owe it to the employer.

Pride in the workplace will strengthen the emotional component of the organizational commitment. Having closer ties means that you become more personally involved. However, on this point it is good to remember that a relationship to an organization is not only about satisfying its needs. Nor is the assessment of what you 'get in return' only about pay. You can gladly commit and make an effort, but you also want reasonable and fair treatment. The organization may expect you to perform certain tasks well, but you might have your own expectations about having influence on how they should be performed. In academic literature the term *psychological contract* is used about the expectations an employee has about reciprocity between himself/herself and the organization.[15] Most of the research in this field has examined the negative consequences when employees experience a breach of the psychological contract. Not surprisingly, the findings point to undermined trust in the organization.[16] We discussed the importance of trust in Chapter 1.

What does a positive mood mean for the organization?

Initially in this chapter we saw examples of employees who expressed positive feelings in the form of pride about their workplace. Research shows that positive feelings and good moods strengthen one's 'self-efficacy,' that is, the individual's belief that their own abilities will be enough. Self-efficacy promotes the idea that you actually *will* manage to perform the tasks you have been assigned. A number of studies also suggest that positive feelings give you more ideas when solving problems, and that they increase your stamina in your job.[17]

What is most interesting in our context, however, is what positive emotions do in terms of colleagues and the organization.[18] Trends found in research suggest that such feelings make people more

- helpful
- engaged
- protective
- constructive

It is important to elaborate on these four keywords. Positive emotions first make people more helpful with their colleagues — often called 'feel good, do good.' The second point refers to a stronger commitment to the organization. This implies that you are willing to sacrifice something — willing to go that extra mile — to promote the organization's interests. The third point shows another approach to the same idea: the will to protect the organization. Specifically, this refers to the fact that you work to ensure that the organization can avoid dangers that might arise. This could refer to accidents, theft, technical problems, or other problems that could arise. The fourth point is clearly and directly relevant for the will to change and innovate: A positive mood in the organization increases the tendency for employees to make constructive proposals. This could mean, for example, proposing improvements in daily practice, reducing waste, improving work quality, and generally coming up with new ideas about changing or developing the organization itself. This does not mean that anyone with objections or protests against ideas for change should be overlooked (see the topic 'tolerance' in the next chapter).

A key term that could have been added to the list above is the tendency employees have *to create goodwill*. While this might be perceived as overlapping with the point about commitment, we should rather see it as being more about what the employee spreads to their surroundings. Examples could include how a good mood or ambience in the work situation makes it more probable that you will praise your workplace to friends and acquaintances, and also to new employees you meet.

Apropos new employees: I have also been a rookie in several workplaces. Some experiences from those times are firmly fixed in my memory: the very first days, where you hardly know how to find the toilet, and have no idea of where to have your lunch. Is there fixed seating? Are the coffee cups private? Can you take milk from the fridge to put in your coffee? In this situation it is really vital that somebody pays attention so you feel welcome. I remember with gratitude and pleasure those who made that extra effort for me. They may be rare in some organizations, but helpers may also suddenly pop up in many situations, even without being asked to do so by their leader.

The somewhat heavy academic expression for this type of action is 'spontaneous' behavior or *extra-role behavior*.[19] The four points on the list above are linked in many ways to this phenomenon. The point is to have a term for important 'extra things' that employees do. These are actions you undertake even if they are not specified in your job description (or are not in agreement with the reward system), but which help the organization to run more smoothly. In my job there are also some tasks that are not described or rewarded formally, but which are still important for the organization.

Several of the themes we have dealt with in this section suggest links between employees' positive feelings and what is called the organization's *corporate reputation*.[20] Most organizations have become increasingly aware of this, even if it can be hard to keep track of it in a world full of demands and expectations. Here a sense of pride will be an advantage, as it can contribute to the positive tendencies described above. Employee pride may therefore also contribute to recruitment, as the idea of becoming a member of the organization will be attractive.

The research on reputation is not *only* interested in an employee's surroundings. Internal circumstances and the organization's 'identity' also come under scrutiny, that is, answering the question about who 'we' are. When people experience that their organization has a strong identity, it helps to bond them together. Thus a feeling of meaning and belonging is generated in a community.[21] According to classic sociology theory, the feeling of belonging has a self-reinforcing effect. When people come to believe they are part of a community, they will interact in such a way that the community is fertilized, cultivated, and strengthened.[22]

Chapter 4

Tolerance

Is diversity appreciated at your workplace? And another question: How well does the organization tolerate failure?

It can be annoying to hear people talk about how tolerant they are because then they are basking in the 'moral radiance' of the tolerant. Seeing it this way, it can be more comfortable to be the tolerant one than the *tolerated one*. In this chapter we will put aside this type of annoyance. Organizations with tolerant features will actually have advantages when it comes to innovation. That is why it is necessary to look into the theme of tolerance.

The idea of tolerance has two meanings in this book. This quotation illustrates the first:

> What is most important is to dare to make mistakes. You cannot manage to create the best products and services faster than your competitors if you do not have high tolerance for failure.[1]

This statement is from an interview with a top leader in banking, talking about the necessity of accepting mistakes and failure. From an academic stance, *tolerance of failure* is very relevant in our context: When we endeavor to accomplish something new, we are in principle stepping into uncharted territory. We cannot know in advance what the outcome of an attempt at innovation will be. Hence the possibility of failure will always be there. It might even be the case that there is *more* chance of failing than succeeding. If there is little tolerance for this in the organization, it will be extremely difficult to work with innovation.

Another important aspect of 'tolerance' emerges in this quotation:

> Are we capable of looking beyond the obvious? Diversity for me is not about what we see, such as dress style, gender or skin color. It's about bringing in different experiences and perspectives. It is in these tensions that innovation and creating something new can take place.[2]

This is the CEO of a construction company talking about her view on diversity. In her reasoning, diversity is a necessary underpinning for innovation and creating something new. She also believes that we should not be blinded by factors such as gender and skin color in this context. We shall return to this. If we are to see diversity as good for an organization, a fundamental *tolerance of difference* is required. This constitutes the second dimension of 'tolerance' in the chapter.

To illustrate this, it may be useful to start with an example:[3]

Optimism as a straitjacket

Around 2000, Nokia was the largest mobile-telephone manufacturer in the world. Its fall from this position could be called the worst belly flop in the industry. What happened?

An in-depth study of the company uncovered a type of *optimism culture*. The strong love affair with optimism manifested itself in the company's middle managers who were very hesitant to present bad news. There was a typical notion that 'if you were too negative it could be your head in the pillory next.' The employees also developed a tendency to avoid asking critical questions, both of their immediate superiors and each other. A middle manager explained: 'Nobody wants to be the one who makes things difficult ... I don't want to be branded as a bad person who criticizes the hard work of others.' Another person pointed out that criticism was seen as only negative; the idea was that if you criticized ongoing work it would be assumed that you were not genuinely devoted. Middle managers also tended to 'create' good news (rather than provide realistic assessments), which could be presented to their superiors. Each product area was required to appear positive about the entity in question if it were to be permitted to continue.

The senior leaders of the company allowed themselves to be seduced by this constant stream of good news. People who criticized and offered negative input were gradually replaced by persons with more optimism in their input and reports. A prevailing tendency was to favor 'new blood' and people with an 'anything is possible' attitude. One middle manager described how the senior executives blindly trusted the young and slick who promised to fix problems. The managerial group did not possess enough knowledge that would have enabled them to assess the technical aspects of the work. They were far more interested in the business plans presented. One senior leader described the situation in this way: 'Many quickly acquired a kind of new technical lingo, becoming quasi-experts. They gave the impression that they knew their business, but I realized (later) that it was only on the surface. Everything was driven by increasingly unrealistic plans and projects. When something went wrong it was ignored or covered up by a dose of good news and quasi-expertise.' In the short term this worked, so the managerial group were able to convince their owners that measures had been initiated to deal with the strategic challenges the organization was facing. This also meant that middle managers kept their jobs, avoided unpleasantness, and kept the divisions busy.

This dominant optimism culture resulted in major problems in the longer term. There was no room to criticize and talk about problems. It simply became difficult to keep up with the developments taking place in mobile-phone technology. Not only did Nokia deliver products of poor quality, but also the products came on the market too late. Nokia's position as world leader was gradually undermined, and the company was eventually taken over by Microsoft.

Thus the optimism culture gave little room for criticizing and discussing problems. Tolerance of failures and flaws was more or less eradicated in this organization. As stated above, this generally results in poor conditions for working with innovation. When mistakes and problems are buried, as they were here, it is also very difficult to learn from them so that the course of the work can be changed or at least adjusted along the way.

The story about Nokia also touches on the theme of diversity. We see that a naive culture developed where only 'certain types of people' were listened to in the organization. The quasi-experts with the gift of the gab and the ability to use the managerial group's business language dominated. People with alternative perspectives and critical technical knowledge who had been part of the decision-making and strategy-planning disappeared. Tolerance for different perspectives will be dealt with more later. First we will examine the topic of diversity in itself.

Job-related diversity

Generally, diversity is a field that can set political sparks flying in a society. Is it possible to take a calm approach to this topic?

At any rate it is not necessary here to adopt particular positions in discussions on politics and measures dealing with equality, immigration, integration, and so on. The position of this book in this field is clear: Diversity is a positive feature for organizations that want to excel at innovation.

Before looking into why this is the case, we should take note of the fact that *the rationale* for diversity in working life has changed over the years.[4] This can be described in three paradigms or phases, where the dominating arguments have been these:

1. Fairness ('the organization should reflect society')
2. Reputation ('customers and users want it')
3. Learning and efficiency ('it is best for the development of the organization')

The first two rationales can both be easily connected to age, gender, and ethnicity. For example, in the first phase it is fair to say that since women constitute half of the population, it is not fair that men fill the large majority of senior management positions. In the second phase, the same argument is applied by pointing to the people for whom the organization exists, namely its customers and users – probably an equal number of women and men, and stating that this should then be reflected in managerial positions.

But the third (and most recent) rationale is the most relevant here, since learning and development are closely connected to innovation and change. But here the newest paradigm can be connected to the previous ones. We can understand a focus on diversity as being fair and good for the organization's reputation, *but at the same time* first and foremost see the rationale just as the CEO at the start of the chapter does: it is good for developing the organization.

Bearing this in mind, I restrict my exploration of diversity here. Factors such as age, gender, and ethnicity will not be explicitly dealt with below. It is also far from certain whether this type of visible or superfluous diversity in fact contributes to enhanced performance in a group.[5]

As our context is organizations and work, the expression *job-related diversity* is more precise.[6] This type of diversity refers to differences in profession, function, skills, and expertise. Many organizations will need to draw on this type of diversity to operate in a reasonable way since their environments and challenges are complex. For some organizations, goals are particularly complex and varied, or even contradictory. For example, a public welfare department will consider the needs of an individual user, but it must also satisfy citizens' demand for equality. Generally, complexity and 'wicked problems' are best met with varied competence.

A more practical aspect of this is that job-relevant diversity strengthens the opportunity for *divergent thinking* in work groups. The fundamental point is that a group in total will far exceed the possibilities of individuals to see a case or a problem from many sides. But this requires that the group is *heterogeneous* (as opposed to homogeneous). This means that it must be diverse so that ideas and perspectives which otherwise would never have come together can indeed be brought together. Such a group will yield more ideas, and these ideas will have greater *variation and originality*. This is beneficial for innovation, where rich access to a good selection of ideas is necessary in all phases of the work.

When the participants in a group provide different types of knowledge, perspectives, and experiences, it is also easier to examine what each individual 'takes for granted' in his or her understanding. This is advantageous in creative work but requires *tolerance of ambiguity*. The idea is that participants must accept that things really can be seen or understood in quite different ways. This does not mean that participants in a group must agree with every way of viewing things. The point is to support and promote *the idea that the world can be understood in different ways.*[7] Carrying this idea a step further is the rather banal (but useful) assumption that other people (professions, competencies, and experiences) 'probably can contribute something.' This attitude is a requirement if job-relevant diversity is to be productive in an organization.

Tolerance for ambiguity may also prevent the negative phenomenon of *group thinking*. This may occur in a group that is under pressure to reach agreement. The phenomenon occurs when objections, critical points of view, and alternative assessments are buried under pressure.[8] There may be many reasons why such a situation occurs. In the previous section we saw how an 'optimism culture' (or fear culture) reduced the possibility of criticizing the development at Nokia. Probably the most famous example of group thinking we can find is the accident involving the space shuttle Challenger in 1986. The leaders in question were so bent on following the launch plan that there was no room for objections. Warnings that cold weather could cause problems with the seals in the booster rocket engines were therefore ignored. The result was that the rocket booster exploded and everyone onboard lost their lives.[9]

Is there a flip side to the coin?

Good arguments for tolerance do not guarantee smooth practice. For example, it can be very annoying to experience conflicting points of view. Here a senior manager in the media industry reflects on the topic:

> If you think like it's so very annoying when this John character always steps up to say that we're doing things the wrong way ... But you have to in fact hear him out; if not there could be ten others like him — who don't care

> or dare to say anything when they see that something is wrong. Because they see that he is ignored or shunned or whatever. And then you have created the ground for allowing us to continue to work in the wrong way.[10]

The message here is that it may be tempting to turn a deaf ear to protests, but that you as the leader must tolerate (and want) critical voices. The consequence would otherwise be that employees will withdraw from the discussion even if they have objections. We remember what happened to Nokia in the story above.

Even if the leader (as the executor of power) has a special responsibility in this context, a similar dynamic may play out between co-workers and in work groups. Therefore job-relevant diversity may cause problems. A group consisting of people with varied backgrounds may be advantageous but will also have a built-in potential for conflict and discontent.[11] The reason is that a broad selection of perspectives may also give several 'competing perceptions' of how work should proceed to satisfy the goals. This disagreement can be productive, of course, but this is conditional on it being used to explore the various action alternatives the group is facing. The group's opportunities will be undermined if the differences lead to personal conflicts and the formation of factions or alliances where the aim is to come out victorious.

Creativity research points out what is required to avoid this problem. The point is that you will hurt yourself and the group if you become *too* focused on your own ideas, because that blocks out the competence of others. A metaphor from association football can be used to explain this: 'It is important to enter the field to be as good as possible yourself. But it is far more important to enter the field to help make your teammates good.'[12] This attitude is well supported by the idea of ambiguity mentioned above, that is, the assumption that others probably have something valuable to contribute to the group if it is to reach its goal.

To gain the advantages that heterogeneously composed groups present, a degree of tension and conflicts must be tolerated. If not, the advantage offered by difference will be poorly exploited. From research on good innovation cultures, we offer this advice: '*Expect and accept conflict,*' '*Accept criticism,*' and '*Don't be too sensitive.*'[13]

It is easier said than done to follow this advice when the level of disagreement and engagement raises the temperature in a discussion where people with quite opposite perspectives are locking horns. It is therefore necessary to have a degree of balance in the diversity so that the distance and differences in perspectives do not increase to the point of being unmanageable. From an empirical study on the development of ideas in work groups, we find the following advice about this balance: 'The participants should have sufficiently different perspectives to create tension in the development of ideas, but the perspective must not be so different that the participants are incapable of understanding each other.'[14] The point is that the differences and the tension level must have their limits if the diversity is to have a positive effect.

It would also be useful if everyone in a heterogeneous group *really agrees on what the goal of the work is.*[15] In football this is probably fairly simple, but more transparent clarifications may be required in groups operating in other contexts. In the wake of the coronavirus pandemic, there is also reason to claim that physical circumstances affect whether participants can benefit from differences in a group. It is easier to exploit the different backgrounds and functions when the group is gathered in the same place than when people are distributed geographically.[16]

To conclude this chapter, we return to the topic that we opened with: tolerance of failure.

Innovation and failure

In a speech given to young people, an aging senior manager offers the following advice: 'Take a chance on falling flat on your face once in a while. If you always want to be safe all the time, you will never go far.' This advice states that it is necessary to assume some *risk* to achieve things.

This is also the case with innovation. Since innovation implies departing (a little or a lot) from what is established, it will involve risk. Thus, the possibility of trouble and failure logically follows. An organization which has zero tolerance for mistakes and failure will not be fit for innovation work. The consequences of this are clearly formulated in research into the question of which cultural norms promote innovation.[17] Two of the tips are:

- *Allow room for trial and error*
- *Don't punish failure or mistakes*

Many leaders will probably agree, particularly those who depend on creation and innovation. However, failing in front of others is sadly an uncomfortable feeling in itself, at work or elsewhere. Most of us feel a bit ashamed of our own mistakes and failure. For leaders wanting to promote the ability to innovate, it is therefore smart to flag these two norms explicitly in the organization. It may be good to admit to one's own failure at times.

There is also a point in thinking about how 'tolerance for mistakes' is *experienced* by the general employee in the organization. This is often what determines how people act in practice. When I discuss this topic with students, they often relate it to their own part-time jobs. They say that it seems as if most managers are aware that it's 'right' to *say* that there's acceptance for mistakes in the company. They want workers (the students) to speak up when they make mistakes, so that the company can avoid any hiding of errors. However, the problem is that students don't *believe* the managers. The part-time workers see that in practice, the one who admits mistakes will face 'silent consequences': for example, they'll be offered fewer opportunities to work attractive shifts. This short classroom report points towards the theme of 'psychological safety,' which will be the subject of the next chapter of the book.

There may also be structures within the organization that indirectly signal the opposite of what is positively communicated by the management. For instance, systems intended to measure actions and results will also carry the message that what is measured is what is important. The individual will then give priority to what is known, established, and countable. The signal the measuring system gives is to choose what is safe rather than what is risky. Obviously these are poor conditions for any kind of experimentation that might lead to innovation. There is reason to be careful when it comes to what measuring and checking job performance *really* tells employees about what the right thing to do is — and what is not the smartest thing to do.[18]

On the other hand, it's possible to signal tolerance for mistakes and failure through more symbolic measures. Here's an example: In the context of fostering innovation within their own organization, a municipality establishes an award called 'Failure of the Year, where the learning itself is what matters.' The award is an attempt to convey an understanding that experimentation and failure are essential for innovation. The addition of the emphasis on learning conveys an interesting message: The aim isn't to celebrate mistakes in general, but to honor those mistakes *that promote learning*.

The main message in this little story is that there are different *types* of failure in an organization. Some are ones we prefer to avoid, while others are necessary for achieving something new. The theme of 'good and bad' failure is therefore worth examining in more detail towards the end of this chapter. In our context, it is useful to distinguish between three types of failure:[19]

A. Basic failures
B. Complex failures
C. Intelligent failures

Basic failures are small and large errors of the 'simple' kind. For example, ordering chicken for dinner at a restaurant but being served beef (due to the waiter entering the wrong item on their terminal). Or an overworked pharmacist giving you medication with a dosage ten times higher than prescribed. The former is trivial while the latter is serious. Basic failures can occur even if we are in a well-known situation. These mistakes can be avoided by being vigilant and precise, and by following established procedures. For instance, the error at the pharmacy would likely have been caught through a procedure of 'double-checking.' This would involve colleagues verifying each other's work before dispensing more serious medications. Of course, these are not the type of mistakes we want to applaud with awards like the one mentioned above.

The second type of failure occurs when the situation is *complex,* hence the term. These errors happen when we are in a more unclear landscape. For example, research shows that a more intricate organization of work can increase the likelihood of accidents.[20] This point can be illustrated by the increasingly extensive use of subcontractors in various industries, such as construction and petroleum. The intention behind such 'outsourcing' often revolves around specialization and optimizing operations. However, this organizational structure makes the situation much more demanding for those involved. People have to deal with multiple companies, actors, or organizations to get the job done. This creates new types of safety challenges.[21]

Then we come to the type of failure that is necessary for innovation, namely *intelligent* failure. These are failures that occur when we take 'calculated' risks and steps into unknown territory. In other words: We want to explore a new opportunity through experimentation. Thus, this is not about 'blind trial and error.' We make explicit and thoughtful assumptions about what we believe *might* work. We minimize the risk of problems and costs, but not so much that we cannot learn as much as possible from the experiment. If we play it safe and stay within the framework of the known, we are unlikely to discover anything new. What we learn from an intelligent failure, we will carry forward in our work and pursuit of improvement and innovation.

It is this last type of failure that the bank manager at the beginning of the chapter is referring to when he wants to introduce new products to his customers. However, we must realize that all types of mistakes and failures will occur in most organizations. This is part of a larger picture that we will delve into in the next chapter.

Chapter 5

Fearlessness

Do you sometimes stop yourself from saying something at work? Let us assume that you are on the brink of bursting out with a question, an idea, or a proposal, but 'something' makes you pull back. Sometimes there are practical and good reasons for dropping what you wanted to say, for example when a meeting is already ten minutes into overtime. Other times, 'something' in the social environment stops people from speaking up. They hold back in fear of the response. If employees experience the working environment in this way, the organization will have a poor starting point for accomplishing change and innovation. This problem can be investigated by means of the concept of *psychological safety*. What does this term mean? How does it work in an organization? We will look more closely into this in this chapter.

In a recent interview, a sports leader was asked about the most important feature of her leadership throughout the years.[1] As a coach, the leader had achieved surprisingly good results in her sport (team handball). The team she coached had had some good results under her predecessor too, but it was only after she took over that the team won one international championship after another. This is what she says about leadership:

> The crucial thing was to understand the resource of each co-worker (player), so that they would start believing they were important. When I was involved initially, it was really quite passive. They had been accustomed to 'being told' what had to be done. I would say that it took four or five years before we settled on the culture where

it is natural and safe to say what you think, and that's the way you contribute with the best of yourself.

What is first obvious is that she looks upon her players as her 'co-workers.' Her narrative develops in an interesting way. Previously, the players' knowledge had not been fully exploited. They had simply not shared their opinions in the group and with the coach (the previous coach). It was not 'safe to say what you thought.' The model she needed to break down and change was: The coach decides and the players perform. We obtain a very good hint about the value of safety in a group here: Knowledge-sharing increased, the safer one felt. She also points out that it took time to change the culture so they had full access to the 'co-worker's resources.' The astonishing results the team achieved under the new coach made her interesting for other coaches and researchers.[2]

Sometimes there is much more at stake than winning in sports. Here is a story from a maternity ward:[3]

Hannah and the twins

The twins that were born this morning came far too early. They appeared to be healthy but were alarmingly small. Giving birth in week 27 meant that the hospital generally considered the case as 'high risk.' But the situation was in capable hands because the ward had a highly competent team on the case: an experienced obstetrician, Martin, with a younger nurse, Hannah, who had just specialized in premature children.

Hannah looks at the tiny twins with concern. She is thinking about the final course in her further education where she was introduced to a newly established 'best practice.' The idea was to give newborns in the 'high risk' category a special medicine that enhances pulmonary development – and to give it as soon as possible. The reason is that premature babies are often born with lungs that are not fully developed; thus they are not always able to breathe on their own outside the uterus. She therefore wonders why the obstetrician has not prescribed this pulmonary medication for these twins. Could he have forgotten to do it? Hannah is just about to remind Martin about this when she realizes that last week she overheard him severely scolding another nurse for questioning a decision he had made. This had occurred right out in the open and was loud and humiliating. Hannah tells herself that the twins will probably cope well; Martin may have good reasons for not using this medication at this moment. He is probably still assessing the case, she thinks. Hannah decides not to make her suggestion. And Martin had already turned on his heels in haste right in front of her. His white coat billowed around him as he hurried off to the next room.

In the story above, we share in Hannah's thoughts where we have turned the tempo down to slow motion. In real time the decision not to say anything to Martin is made in a split second. Furthermore, she is probably not fully aware of the decision she is making. Two issues are in play here. On the one hand, there is the risk of being humiliated by Martin. On the other hand, there is the possibility that the twins actually need this pulmonary medication to ensure their good development. Hannah has told herself that the obstetrician knows better than her, and also that her input will hardly be welcome. More or less consciously, she has weighed the immediate risk (her humiliation) as being more significant than the *more* serious possibility that lies in the future (the poor development of the twins). We will examine two reasons for this outcome.

First, Hannah's more or less conscious choice is not surprising, even if it is unfortunate. The human tendency to prioritize the here and now over future events is generally known from the fields of economics and psychology.[4] The phenomenon may explain some apparently illogical actions, such as why people buy on credit well aware that their financial prospects are poor, or why many people grab that 'extra piece of chocolate' even though they actually want to lose weight. The story above is somewhat 'invisible,' and thus overlooked as an example of this problematic bent, namely that Hannah should have said something but holds her tongue to avoid consequences there and then.

Second, we know from classic sociology that people in general put a lot of effort into controlling the impression that others in their surroundings have of them.[5] The image of ourselves that we want to present will vary according to the situation and the role we 'play.' It is not very demanding to sit in your living room and watch cartoons with your family. But as a rule, we normally set other demands on how we appear in a job context. Nurse Hannah's silence stems from her fear that she will appear annoying, ignorant, and incompetent, which in turn is a result of her social environment. A situation without this fear would have been far better. This is where research on psychological safety enters the picture.

What is psychological safety?

The above example from the maternity ward is based on the book *The Fearless Organization*, written by Harvard professor Amy Edmondson. Published in 2019, it has already gained recognition inside and outside the world of research. The author's main project is to show how 'psychological safety' at the workplace strengthens the ability to learn and innovate in organizations. Psychological safety is defined as the belief that the working environment is so safe that you dare to express yourself and be yourself. It can be explained more precisely in this way:

> When people experience psychological safety in their workplace, they feel safe enough that they can share concerns and mistakes without fear of being punished or being embarrassed. They are confident that they can express opinions without being humiliated, ignored or subjected to ridicule. They also know that they can ask questions when they are unsure about something. They tend to trust and respect their colleagues.[6]

The definition makes it tempting to look back at the coach of the handball team. It took a long time to get the players to offer their opinions. One thing was that the team needed to change an ingrained habit. But the players also needed to feel that their input would not lead to a lot of eye-rolling, for example from experienced teammates. Even worse (from the players' point of view): Could disagreeing with the coach leave you warming the substitutes' bench?

The more dramatic story about the twins ended happily. The newborn twins fortunately coped well without the pulmonary medication — this time. What if Hannah had worked in a hospital where she felt psychologically safe? Then we could envision that she would not have hesitated to discuss the need for pulmonary medication with the doctor. It would have felt so natural that she would immediately have spoken up. Hannah would have taken it as given that it was okay to ask the question, even though it might not lead to medication being given to the twins.

In a climate with psychological safety, Martin would have responded by explaining why he thought the twins did not need medication or would have written a prescription for the medication if he agreed with Hannah. The outcome for the ward would at any rate have been good. The patients would have received the necessary medication, and/or the team would have learned something about the treatment of premature babies. Leaving the room under such circumstances, we can envision that Martin would have thanked Hannah for her input. He would be aware that she would always speak up if she was wondering about something.

Having psychological safety in the ward does not, however, refer only to individual relationships, but also to the environment or *climate* in the section. Therefore we may infer: Knowing that she would be taken seriously, Hannah could have contacted her leader. She could have proposed a new policy in the ward to add her newly acquired knowledge. In this way, considering pulmonary medication for premature babies could become a new, permanent part of the treatment.

The key point is that psychological safety prevents and reduces the type of *silence* the story about the twins demonstrates. When people offer their opinions, the conditions for open and genuine communication are improved. This will shed light on problems and mistakes and uncover the need for change, thus providing a platform for increased knowledge-sharing, improvement of practice, and dissemination of ideas, which may inspire innovation. Systematic review of the research on psychological safety shows that these effects are well documented.[7]

Is it mostly about being nice and kind?

The phenomenon of psychological safety has been studied over several decades in various types of organizations, such as hospitals, schools, private businesses, and public administration. The interest in this research and the phenomenon is widespread, both inside and outside the world of research. Along the way, some misunderstandings of the concept have arisen, leading to the need to clarify what 'psychological safety' actually *is*, as well as what it is *not*. Here are four useful clarifications:[8]

1. Psychological safety is *not* about agreeing to be nice and kind. The point is rather that the environment is open to productive disagreement through the exchange of views. One *does not* necessarily need to have a relaxed and cozy environment to have a psychologically safe place.
2. Psychological safety is *not* a personality trait. Thus it does not really matter whether a person is extroverted or introverted. On the contrary, the phenomenon refers to the *climate* at the workplace. All in all, this climate affects individuals quite equally, regardless of personality.
3. Psychological safety is *not* about lowering work requirements. You can have a workplace with high work standards that is also psychologically safe. High requirements combined with fear obviously do not make a good mix, putting each employee under intense pressure.
4. Psychological safety is *not* the same as trust, even if these two are related. The main difference is that psychological safety is experienced on the *group level*. In practice this means that people who work together will have fairly similar perceptions as to whether they are working in a psychologically safe climate or not. Trust is more focused on specific people, systems, or organizations. You may, for example, trust one co-worker to do his or her job, while not having much trust in another.

It should be added that while psychological safety describes an immediate here-and-now experience, trust is more about something in the future. When nurse Hannah remains silent in front of the obstetrician, it is because she fears humiliation *there and then*. Trust is more about whether she believes the obstetrician is able and willing to provide good treatment for the patients.

Psychological safety is a solid foundation

As stated above, there is clear evidence that psychological safety is positive for various types of organizations.[9] This obviously does not mean that everything is top notch if only this is in place. It can rather be described as a sensible *foundation* which will make it easier for the organization to reach its goals.

How do employees describe such a foundation of safety? I acquired an introspective and realistic picture of this in a recently completed research project. The goal of the project was to encourage employee-initiated innovation in municipal healthcare services.[10] The plan was that the employees from four workplaces would take part in training, activities, and testing of new ideas over the course of a year. As researchers, we were very pleased when we saw that a good number of concrete innovations emerged from this activity. Admittedly, the results were unevenly distributed; some of the workplaces had succeeded in introducing many new things, while others had fewer concrete results.

Seen in the light of research on psychological safety, another outcome of the project was at least as interesting: The feeling of safety at all four workplaces had developed positively during the project period.[11] What did this mean in practice for the employees? Here are some typical statements from the participants in a survey conducted anonymously after the project:

- 'More employees feel more included, so it's easier to say what's on your mind.'
- 'There is more room now to propose changes.'
- 'No longer is it just the loudest voices and the bold ones that get heard.'

- 'There's a better sense of togetherness, where people are not afraid to propose new ideas.'
- 'We trust each other more, and there is less difference between the skilled and the unskilled workers.'

Looking back, this positive development is perhaps more important than the improvements themselves, because the premises for succeeding in the future have been strengthened. These statements suggest that both the fear culture and the sense of hierarchy have been reduced, and that there is 'greater room' for proposing ideas and suggesting something new. No longer are only the bravest and most highly educated heard. When more individuals feel included so they can participate with their knowledge, the potential for change and innovation obviously increases. The next step will be to exploit this foundation to develop and prepare services of good quality. With increased psychological safety at the four workplaces, the job has probably become easier to accomplish now. However, it must be added that psychological safety is not a state that a work environment achieves once and for all, but rather something that must be maintained (or recreated) over time.[12]

Fearlessness opens for thinking out loud and asking odd questions

We have seen that psychological safety opens up opportunities in the organization. For example, the foundation has been built for learning from mistakes and failure, and also for benefiting from the diversity of the organization's knowledge base (see the previous chapter). Psychological safety will contribute to developing an innovation culture. The reason is that it is easier to realize *attitudes that promote innovation.*[13] Here are some examples, in this case formulated as preferred norms, or perhaps 'traffic rules':

- Appreciate and protect ideas
- Respect unfinished and emergent ideas
- Encourage different types of thinking
- Promote open and inclusive communication

The point is that a workplace with psychological safety is a place where you can start *thinking out loud*. Not least, it is a place where you can ask *questions* about what is taken for granted in the organization. This may refer to anything from overarching strategy to specific routines and embedded ways of working. Such questions can function as tools for developing the organization further and are particularly potent when it comes to innovation.

Before proceeding with this topic, I will stop for just a moment. I have been in working life so long that I *know* that some will be a little upset (or exhausted) when they read the previous section. Perhaps some will think, 'Does everything always need to be changed or developed?' or 'We also need peace and stability to take care of what we have.' I have two responses to this. The first is that this chapter is about having a good foundation for changing and creating something new *if or when* it is necessary. The second is a reminder that I am not referring to just any organization in this book. 'The dream organization' is tailor-made for those who want better opportunities for change and innovation.

I return to the point about being open to asking questions: Several researchers focus on how *certain types of question* may have an important function when trying to initiate innovation.[14] Particularly, so-called divergent questions are interesting. These are open questions exploring, expanding, or developing something. This type of question will typically start with 'how,' 'why,' or 'which possibilities,' and so on. As seen from the perspective of innovation research, divergent questions can be categorized into the following:[15]

- *Dumb or naive questions.* These questions may appear to be dumb because they ask about something everyone knows, or should we say, *thinks* they know.
- *Wild questions.* These are questions that appear to be so strange that people tend to not take them seriously. The point is that dumb or wild questions may lead to new thoughts and ideas. Moreover, they may give birth to *new* questions that can be really sharp and good.
- *Impossible questions* are those that are asked even though everyone knows they are not feasible, that they are basically impossible. Even so, it might be important to ask these questions because they challenge what is taken for granted, thus possibly leading to new ideas.
- *Burning questions* are valuable for creating motivation in the work of innovation. These are questions stemming from matters of burning interest in an innovation process. They focus on matters employees really want to explore and tackle.
- *Hypothetical questions* have the advantage that they focus on new opportunities. What if ...? Can we envision that ...? Would it be possible to ...?

We quickly understand that most of these questions would probably never be asked if the employee feared being ridiculed, humiliated, or ignored. Without psychological safety the access to this type of thinking out loud is closed to an organization. It must also be added that circumstances may vary quite widely in an organization. In reality there may be valuable 'pockets' (large or small groups) where psychological safety is prevalent. These may exist in parallel with other groups more dominated by a lack of safety.

The example from the social healthcare service in the previous section is also interesting in light of the list above. The participants gradually experienced greater safety at their workplace. We, as researchers, heard an increase in divergent questions as the project continued.[16] Some were related to the content of the job; for example: Why are we putting so much focus on just these tasks? Are we giving priority to the right things? Also, not least, the burning question: What is *really* most important for our users?

What about the creative dictators?

It is fitting to conclude the chapter by asking a somewhat bold question. How can some organizations achieve great success *even though* their leaders are both arrogant and 'dictatorial,' and create insecurity around them?

Amy Edmondson says that she is often asked about this.[17] The query is often accompanied by a concrete example of a company that has achieved success but without psychological safety. These are her comments:

- We cannot disregard that the success is due to the leadership, *but* it may just as much be due to other particularly favorable circumstances, or possibly pure luck.
- Could the success have been greater if there was increased psychological safety in the organization? We will never know.
- How long will the success last? Will the organization manage to change when needed? Will skillful employees leave in the long run?

Steve Jobs is an example of a leader who was quite dictatorial, but who still enjoyed great success (with Apple). In fact, his biographer described Jobs as 'the worst boss in the world,' someone who could be directly terrifying to people.[18] Edmondson calls Jobs a rare genius who had abnormally good instincts. Not least, he was unique in that he would specify in detail what others had to do to realize his own ideas.

The conclusion is therefore that geniuses are very rare. For the rest of us, Jobs' approach is not recommended. Not being geniuses, we cannot afford to overlook the human resources found in the organization. Rather, our success depends on employees who fearlessly bring their knowledge and ideas to the table.

Chapter 6

Practical Anchoring

Have you been involved in a 'change project' or two where you are working? It is quite probable you have. It is also quite probable that the project failed in achieving its goals. Statistics from research prove this: There is *a lot* of change in working life, and there is a lot of *unsuccessful* change.[1] In this chapter I will examine one of the reasons why change projects fail.

The starting point for this chapter is a long-term research project on change in organizations. I was part of this project, which for simplicity's sake I will call the 'CO project' in this book.[2] The results from the CO project point out what is difficult when working to accomplish change. One of the most striking findings is that employees experience the change work as *distant from their practice*. The study shows that this has a number of unfortunate consequences. The most obvious one is that possible improvements in practice come to nothing, as the planned changes fail to be relevant and useful. At times, it can actually be even worse, when the changes that are introduced make it *more difficult* (not easier) to do a good job. Solutions remote from practice also reduce the employees' interest in engaging with the next change project. Thus the organization's ability to change is undermined.[3]

I am not claiming that efforts to introduce change should only deal with practical matters. Then it would not be easy to achieve something new. The point in this chapter is that organizations strengthen their ability to change if the employees experience the changes as relevant. More specifically, it must be perceived that plans, initiatives, and projects are *grounded* in the work that is actually to be performed. This is what the heading 'Practical Anchoring' refers to.

We will start by examining an example where things really go awry:[4]

One hundred days in the corner office

Henry was both surprised and happy when the message came: he got the job! He had kept this thought to himself, but he believed that the company did not adequately focus on younger leader talents, like him. Now he would show them. As the new leader of the development department he was going to transform it into something far more dynamic, and in record time. When he received the formal offer, he asked for 100 days' grace. The managing director nodded appreciatively to his wish.

Henry had decided to use his time well. First he allocated himself a large corner office where he could sit undisturbed and plan his start as leader. Then he hired a well-known consultancy firm to study the department and propose improvements. In the department, people started talking. Everyone knew they had a new boss, but few had seen that much of him. Consultants came and went. And the questions they asked in interviews created concern and rumors about what was going on. After more than a month, a curious employee spokesperson knocked on the door of the corner office. The talk was short. 'Wait and see,' Henry said, smiling broadly, 'wait and see!'

Henry was excited when the new organization plan at long last was finished. He noted that the auditorium was full. His presentation went well, and he interpreted the absence of questions as a mix of respect and support. The next day, the managing director came to Henry's office wanting to know what had happened. He had heard that the department was seething with protests and unrest.

Henry calmly explained that some resistance to change was to be expected. 'It is both natural and human, so when somebody wants to accomplish something, the thing is that everyone has to be patient and hang in there.'

After two months there had been little change. People were apparently working the same way as before. It appeared that they were ignoring Henry's plan, in spite of his increasingly angry exhortations. Eventually, other departments started to complain about decreasing quality in the services supplied by the development department. Six months later, a new leader of the department was appointed.

This story should be kept in mind while reading this chapter. One detail must be clarified right away: Why was Henry given permission from the managing director who hired him when he asked for his 100 days? The explanation is that the managing director had done the same thing the last time *he* started in a new managerial role. Later, Henry would learn that the managing director had spent his hundred days on something very different from making a grand plan. He had used this time to systematically talk with his new subordinates. He wanted to know about and understand the work they were doing. This would inform his leader role in the time ahead. The managing director would probably have been surprised if he had known how Henry was planning to spend his hundred days.

Things rarely go as badly as in this example. Even so, it is not uncommon that leaders (or groups of leaders) think too much and too long on their own *before* they bring in the people to initiate the planned changes. In research on making changes in organizations, it has also been typical for leaders to see the organization from the 'top down' (in other words, from a pure leadership perspective).[5] This becomes too narrow-minded and therefore problematic. The world appears quite different looking from the 'top down' than it does when looking from the 'bottom up,' that is, where the workers are.

One thing Henry did not understand was that he would need *contributions from several perspectives* to achieve change in practice. His approach was like wearing a patch over one eye: you lose depth perception, your steps falter, and you lose touch with the ground.

So how does planned change appear from below? We will look at this in the next section.[6]

The voices from the floor

In the above-mentioned CO project, we studied relatively large organizations. It is of course easier to experience distance between 'us on the factory floor' and 'the leaders' when the context is a large organization rather than a small firm. If all the employees can gather together around a table, talk about change and development can easily arise. In that case,it is much less likely that solutions 'far removed from practice and change' will be introduced. However, the conditions do not need to be much larger before this can become a problem. Attaching importance to good anchoring of change activities in practice is therefore relevant for all organizations of any considerable size, irrespective of industry and sector.

The workers we interviewed in the CO project (the informants) have no connections to the company in the example above. However, what they have to say can illuminate some of what occurred in the department where Henry was made leader. Our informants often called new leaders 'new brooms,' which in itself implies distancing. Skepticism was tangible when the talk focused on typical leader changes, such as in this statement:

> When a new boss arrives, he of course needs to assert himself. Some new tricks are needed to show to his bosses. So it's a requirement that you show your superiors that you're doing something. I think there's something there. They're not real business leaders anymore. It's become too academic, in a way.

We do not know whether Henry's grand plan was only done for show for 'his bosses.' The point is, however, that what is done may easily *be understood this way* by the workers. We do not need to applaud this informant's nostalgic feelings about 'proper business leaders,' but we can see that the expectations around a change in leaders are not very positive. When Henry isolates himself in his office for a hundred days to prepare his grand plan for change (his 'new tricks'), he confirms these negative expectations. In the CO project, we also observed that the *content* of change plans could appear to be quite thin. Here is an informant telling us about his encounter with a change project:

> It's been difficult to come to grips with what this change project really is. There is a gap between visions and practice. There has been no lack in the volume of information. There has been a hailstorm of PowerPoints, but there is hardly anything concrete, and few pegs to hang things on.

What is presented appears to be abstract and remote to this employee. Other informants use more acerbic terms, calling the planned changes 'smoke and mirrors.' They are not related to known facts, and thus have very little meaning. Thus it is hard to see any links between the plans and the day-to-day work. We do not know whether 'the pegs' were primarily missing from Henry's grand plan. But we do know that he did not make his plan in collaboration with the professionals working in the department. This makes it very hard to create good links between the plan and what actually goes on in practice. A third informant points precisely to the problem of having too little contact with the planners:

> The people running things ... they don't know what they really decide. There are too many economists sitting and making decisions believing that they know how things work. They should have come closer 'further down' and checked before they made decisions.

We do not need to fixate on a particular group (economists), which is the target here. The claim that the decision-makers fail to see the consequences of their own decisions is more interesting. The reason is that they lack insight. The diagnosis says that the decision-makers *believe* that they know enough. The prescribed medicine is to find out how the work 'further down' in the organization is done. To be fair, it should be mentioned that Henry made an attempt to 'check' the practice. He hired consultants to interview his employees.

In the introduction I used the terms 'practical anchoring' and 'grounding' about change actions that build on insight into what is done in practice. For Henry this would have required him to spend far more time out of his corner office. If he had done this, his plan could have included more knowledge about the day-to-day practice in the department. That means more and more *in-depth* knowledge than the consultants managed to obtain. This would have been reasonable, regardless of whether it was precisely the practice he wanted to change over time.

In both the CO project and in the example with Henry, change plans trigger *resistance* among the employees. This is, of course, annoying for leaders who want to introduce change.

It is just as annoying for employees who are looked upon as unwilling and difficult when they protest. There is reason to examine further the theme of 'resistance to change,' because this is where the shoe pinches.

The leaders' understanding of resistance

In the book *Lethal Changes*, the author writes about his visit to a major company (the name is anonymized).[7] He has an appointment with the director, who talks enthusiastically about a change project he has started. The enthusiasm is somewhat surprising because the project has run up against heavy resistance from knowledgeable people in the enterprise. Several employees have even threatened to resign in critical letters in the local newspaper. For this reason the author would like to discuss with the director how to find good ways of handling the problems. But the director has no doubts about his strategy, which he explains briefly in this way:

> My job is to cover my ears until they have stopped screaming. Sooner or later everybody will see this as a success.

We will not pursue this specific case further here. The point is to examine the director's take on resistance. What logic lies behind his thinking? We will see that research literature in this field virtually *invites* leaders to think in this way. Here is the explanation.

A well-known model from organizational psychology illuminates reactions to change and restructuring according to the idea of 'experiences of loss.'[8] This theory is taken from research into traumatic events. From such a perspective it will be logical to see resistance as a 'natural' reaction. You react since you are losing something of value. Changes that are underway make you uncertain about the future. Do I have the competence required for what's coming? What will my role be now? Who am I to work with?

The experience of loss may be compared to grief reactions. Let us look at an example of a model for change based on this.[9] Here the reactions of an individual are divided into four phases:

1. Denial
2. Resistance
3. Exploration
4. Attachment

The first two phases of the model deal with the past (before change), while the last two concern the future (after change). The denial phase is typically one where employees do not want to admit that change is coming, and they therefore work as before. The resistance phase will be dominated by uncertainty and loss of control. Here emotional reactions such as anger and anxiety can be expected, possibly also direct sabotage of what is new. But then, after some time, comes the exploration phase. Here people try to fill the new roles introduced by the change, and endeavor to establish new relationships. Testing and experimenting may characterize this phase. Finally the attachment phase comes. Now the new roles are accepted, and people begin to identify with the new organization. Collaboration towards a common goal has now started.

A number of models for employee reactions to change have a similar development: moving from a 'normal state' to imbalance and then to a new normality.[10] This is often linked to the idea that while work morale and effectiveness temporarily decline when the normal state of affairs is disturbed, the curves rise again, and then move to a higher level than before the change.

There may be *something* to think about with this type of model. Change can doubtlessly cause uncertainty and a sense of loss. But there are problematic aspects to these models. First, they are based on a predetermined final state. It is assumed that endorsement of 'the new' *will come* sooner or later. There is clearly no guarantee that this will actually be the case. Second, the models have a 'paternal' aspect to them. It is assumed that the (unknowing) employees will accept and support the change once they 'have had time to think about it.' It is like an angry child who has been told to stand in the corner until it has calmed down.

We now see that these models for change and resistance actually lend indirect support to the director in the last example. His change strategy was to cover his ears until the employees had had their tantrum. He apparently thinks that 'it is only natural that people protest. They don't understand. They feel loss and uncertainty, and they are in a grief process. Eventually they will open up and accept the new situation.' However, as it turned out, the road ahead was not that smooth for this change project.[11]

There are many reasons for resistance

A widespread attitude is to see resistance from employees as irritating and negative — something primarily 'blocking the road' to change. We find this both in research literature and in more popular science books about change management.[12] The person who is *pro* change is often portrayed in positive terms, while the skeptic is seen as hostile or poor at tackling change. The focus is therefore on how to get as many employees as possible to let go of their resistance, for example by persuading them, or by waiting and letting them process their sense of loss. What then gets lost in this view is that the *content* of the change could be fueling the resistance. Perhaps the change may have unintended negative consequences in practice? Change activities should therefore be anchored to some degree in practice.

The major weakness in the models in the previous section is that they fail to realize the following possibility: The protesters *may have good intentions and useful objections* on behalf of the enterprise. Employees have knowledge that is not as easily available to change managers. This is knowledge about how proposed changes will affect the possibility of doing a good job for the organization. Knowledge about the practical work 'on the floor' should therefore be seen as a resource in the change work.[13] Resistance may be an expression of important insight that must be included in a change project. There must also be an option that can address the fact that the change project *might* prove to be an ill-conceived idea and that it should therefore be scrapped.

It is useful and necessary to realize that there may be different reasons for resistance.[14] Here are some examples:

a. Fear of the unknown
b. Loss of personal goods or benefits
c. Loss of influence
d. Loss of relationships
e. Broken expectations
f. Professional disagreement over solutions
g. Extra work or doubling of work
h. Negative consequences for one's own practice (or the organization as such)

Anyone working with change should therefore not be too hasty in concluding what the underlying reasons for the resistance are. It is problematic if leaders become fixated on the first example above, concluding that 'people do not like change regardless,' end of story. We have also seen that the next three examples in the list (b–d) dominate in some research literature, where the idea is that resistance is primarily a reaction to loss. But the point here is to never disregard the more practice-based reasons, as seen in examples f–h. This means accepting the following: that resistance may be based on solid expertise relating to what is best for the organization, and about what will work best in practice.

Practical anchoring in the change work

There is little doubt that changes with no anchoring in practice may have a negative impact of great significance for an organization. To illustrate the wide scope of this issue, we will conclude this chapter by looking at two examples from quite different organizations.

> (1) When a local authority built a new office-building, they introduced an open-office solution without permanent places for their employees. The office arrangement also had an adjoining café and separate meeting rooms with glass walls. The problem was that the new concept also included employees who worked in the local authority's child welfare service. The offices were very poorly suited to the practical work of this department. The processing of confidential information was difficult, and the glass cages were not suitable for meetings with stressed and vulnerable clients. Whenever confidential telephone calls came in, the consultants had to leave their place and look for a vacant quiet room. The toilets were even used as a backup for confidential phone calls.

In this case it was strikingly obvious that the changes lacked 'grounding' in what type of work was being done in practice.[15]

In other situations, the consequences become more visible and insidious. Here is an example from a customer service center in an insurance company.[16]

(2) In an attempt to improve operations, a simplified system was introduced where employees were measured and rewarded according to the number of telephone calls carried out per hour. The idea was to process (i.e. insure) customers as rapidly and effectively as possible. The system turned out to have an effect, leading to increased sales. However, problems arose. The company was unable to keep their new employees. The practice in this section had been that experienced sales personnel trained new employees, as in an apprentice scheme. But the newly introduced measuring system meant that established sales personnel gave priority to answering incoming calls above all else. The interest in training new co-workers disappeared. New sales staff were seen more like potential competitors in the new system (why help a competitor?). The new employees no longer succeeded in this environment and therefore quit quite quickly.

These two examples help to illuminate changes that do not take into consideration how the work is performed in practice. After the critical review in this chapter you may be thinking, 'Personally I would never change anything at all out of respect for the good work being done.' I hope this is not the impression you are left with. If the local authority had considered the needs of the child welfare service, they would have avoided many problems and frustrations. The customer service center above also had unnecessary problems, having 'forgotten' an essential part of the work of the sales staff. The point is to improve the change process, not to avoid all change. Most organizations do not really have a realistic choice. It can be said, undeniably, that organizations have a *built-in inertia* which means that they change more slowly than required by their surroundings.[17] To keep up, it is therefore necessary to undertake some changes once in a while, willingly or not.

To stay anchored in practice in the change work, knowledge about the current practice is necessary. Then 'change leaders' and 'practicians' (ordinary employees) will find common arenas for sharing knowledge about practice and about the need for change. Roughly speaking, this part of the change work may be envisioned in a recurring sequence:

A. Common discussion on what can or should be done
B. Testing something out
C. Joint discussion about how things went
D. Back to A (if needed)

This model means that ordinary employees are included early on in a change process, even as early as when the plans for change are still at the ideas stage. Resistance and objections can then be voiced right at the initial stage (point A). This work method circles around *experimentation* (point B), with subsequent *assessment* (point C). Thus it is open to *breaks* from established practice – in other words innovation in the organization and its work methods.

You may perhaps object that this appears to be work intensive and time consuming. But bear in mind that this effort will probably be rewarded by more relevant and workable changes in the long term. When the changes are experienced as relevant by those concerned, a positive side effect is also achieved: It is more interesting to become engaged in the next change project. In the final stage, it may turn out that the whole change process has gone faster than anticipated. Even if you devote much more effort early on in the process, you will earn this back when the new practice has its debut.[18]

Chapter 7

Genuine Participation

Imagine the following: Changes are in the air at your workplace. The situation is presented as 'open,' and you are asked to engage in the process. But eventually you start to feel that the hand has already been dealt, and that it does not really matter what you do or say. Therefore you have probably been the victim of 'false participation.' This does not necessarily mean that there is a secret and evil plan behind what is taking place. But it is still frustrating, both for you and the organization. When employees experience something like this, the organization's ability to change and innovate is undermined. This chapter deals with the importance of 'genuine participation.' The participation must be real, and it must be *perceived* as such by those involved.

Even if this topic is quite serious, I will start with a humorous story told by a leader in a podcast interview.[1]

The notebook

When people at work are hassling you, it's typical that bosses will say things like 'Sure, this is a great idea, so we'll be looking into it.' Well ... I had a boss once and do you know what he would do when people were griping? There was one lady in particular who complained a lot about her job. And every time she came to a meeting with him he took out a notebook. He took out the notebook and a pen. Then he pretended that he was sitting and making notes of everything she said. As the meeting progressed he would say such things as 'Yes, that's a really good idea, very good input' and 'Hold it, say that again, I just need to note it down.' And after the meeting he simply put the book away again (until the next meeting), but he never did anything more about it. But I think she really felt that she was heard.

I am not sure whether this story is 100 percent true or not. At any rate it is both comical – and nasty. But there is an important point here. For an impatient leader, it can sometimes be tempting to pretend that there is genuine participation. In the Nordic countries most employees expect to be heard and to have some influence on their job.[2] This requires time, energy, and attentiveness on the part of leaders.

Overall, working life in the Nordic countries is characterized by the low power-distance between leaders and employees.[3] It is *common* for employees to have some influence on decisions. Over time, a culture has emerged of participation and collaboration between leaders and their employees. And there is little doubt that this benefits both parties: It is easier to achieve positive, constructive, and effective relationships between leaders and employees. Research in this field also shows that participation has a positive impact on job satisfaction and turnover. Another effect is also well documented: It increases the probability of succeeding in the organization's efforts to change.[4]

This means that participation is a valuable capital for the organization. Of course capital needs to be managed in a reasonable way so that it is not drained or dismantled. This is where the risk of false participation enters the picture. The long-serving CEO of Statoil/Equinor (a large energy company) offered the following warning in a recent interview on leadership:

> We have learned in our working life that anchoring decisions is the most effective way of getting things done.

> But if you're going to run a process in the organization, the intention has to be honest. You simply have to *want* to hear what people think; pretending just does not cut it – because then you have ruined the possibility of anchoring the process. You cannot have both an open and a closed process, it's either-or.[5]

Here we see that it is presented as self-evident that participation is part of the most rational way to practice change work in a Nordic setting. Perhaps knowing this is what leads this executive to warn against false participation. If something appears to be virtually 'obligatory,' it may easily slip into a kind of formality, something merely ticked off on the 'list of things to be done' before moving on to the 'real' work. The reasoning here is that leaders must make a choice: Either you invite workers into a participation process or you do not. And if you invite them, then the invitation must be genuine, which means that you must spend time and listen carefully. If the game is false, the possibility of successful change is lost.

How does false participation work in practice?

Now let us look at some examples that are far less caricatures than the introductory story about the notebook. Bearing in mind the quotation from the former Statoil CEO, we will stay offshore. Here an employee in the company talks about his experience of a major change project:

> In the latest reorganizations I have felt that the agenda is stuck where it is. You could offer a lot of input. But the agenda which was here from the start is still there when the whole project is finished. Little consideration is given to the employees. The final decision has been made at an early stage. The employees are included just for show. They hear what you have to say, but they do things as they

> planned earlier. There is a requirement that employees have to be included in a major restructuring – which is what we have been through. But it appears that it's game over and the decisions have been made at an early point in time ... Little trust is put in new change projects due to experiences with earlier projects.[6]

The starting point for this story is a specific project that led to changes in administration and the way they were organized. We see that the informant generalizes about what has happened. The feeling of having been involved in something 'just for show' has been a recurring theme in the change work. He also points out the consequences of these experiences. It is expected that the same thing will happen (again) when the next change project is on the horizon. In his case, we are talking about experiences with large projects, which probably heightens the sense of powerlessness – or the feeling that 'your hand has been dealt' somewhere far away.

On the other hand, we do not need to be talking about large and complex projects to see the phenomenon of false participation and the accompanying feelings of resignation. We will now look at some examples from interviews with employees working with offshore catering (including food and housekeeping).[7] Here a cleaner talks about being consulted for advice:

> We actually said that it was impossible to have white floor covering. But they bought it anyway, on sale, and someone had said it was so fine and light-looking. So the idea that we are included, give advice and take part in decisions – I don't really know about that. We participate in meetings, and they don't listen to us. That's always the same. So there was no point in us taking part in the meeting, as it turned out.

The experience of the decision concerning floor covering is a specific example of a more general pattern this informant sees. She doubts whether there is really any point in participating in the meetings. Other co-workers show even clearer irritation. Below, two employees talk about their experiences.

The first informant is tired of what she perceives as hypocrisy. The gap is wide between what is said and what is done:

> You really don't mean anything to them. They say, 'You have to tell us, you have to tell us,' but it's propaganda and gibberish. They don't listen anyway.

> The feeling we were left with then, after this committee, was that we were only there so the leader could have documentation of employee participation, and that's it!

The second quotation offers a clear point of view on what is going on. It is required that participation is documented, and that was the *real* reason she had been included in the committee's work. She is virtually a hostage in this situation — the leader's alibi when documenting participation — while participation was not what the involved parties had experienced.

The next informant talks about what the consequences of such a practice will be:

> It comes to a point where you don't want to get involved anymore. That you spend too much energy on it. The consequence is that we come out here and do our job, and nothing more. Because it turns out time after time that there's no point in getting involved. Many of us feel like this.

The above informants suggest that their experiences are *typical*, that unfortunately they are not exceptions to the rule. Nor is the problem unfamiliar to researchers who have studied change efforts in large Norwegian organizations: They call this phenomenon 'fake involvement,' and it is discussed precisely as something that will undermine employees' real involvement in change work.[8] The researchers state that this phenomenon has surfaced in almost all change processes they have studied (very many indeed). Other studies have also identified this problem, calling it 'pseudo-participation.'[9] The consequence recurring in all these studies is that if employees' expectations about genuine participation are not met, disappointment, frustration, and 'withdrawal' will be the result.

It is interesting to note that the phenomenon is not particularly visible in international research.[10] One reason may be that such research (generally) is performed in settings that are completely different from the Nordic ones. In the Nordic countries most employees expect to have an influence on their job, and their leaders generally understand and accept this. The quotations above show how individuals react when these expectations are not met.

What is at stake?

Considering all the statements from employees in the previous section, the objection could be raised that we are only looking at the case from one side. Nor can we ignore the fact that the leaders may have had *intentions* of establishing genuine participation. The point, however, is that the employees are left with these negative perceptions. If those in charge of the change work are unable to leave a better impression than this, the organization is going to develop a problem. This problem has three consequences, which we will examine in order:

1. Undermined capacity for change
2. Undermined innovation ability
3. Poorer quality in decisions

1. The concept of 'change capacity' may be defined as 'the ability of organizations to change *while also* maintaining day-to-day operations.'[11] Here is where the classical dilemma between operation and development raises its head. Organizations cannot focus *too* much on change and innovation as they must keep the wheels of their daily operations turning. The reactions of employees to change is one of the factors that determine the ability to change. It is therefore reasonable to assert that any work to introduce changes that has given people the experience of false participation will undermine the capacity to change.

Research also points out that this type of negative experience can be spread through stories the employees tell each other. This then can lead to 'cold' or *cynical attitudes to change* spreading in the organization's culture.[12] Employees 'rolling their eyes' at new change initiatives will not make it easy to engage in the further work. There is a familiar expression for what happens when changes are given the cold shoulder: The so-called BOHICA effect means that employees do not care about continuing attempts at change ('Bend Over, Here It Comes Again').[13]

2. There is little doubt that false participation has a negative effect on the internal (intrinsic) motivation of employees because they have taken part in change work which they have experienced as meaningless. There are strong indications that people become less creative when their internal motivation is weakened.[14] Creativity (such as new ideas) is obviously a necessary ingredient for innovating successfully. The consequence is, then, that false participation undermines the employees' ability to innovate in an enterprise.

To exploit the full potential for innovation in an organization, you are dependent on having the employees on the floor with you. The person who is closest to a task is the one who can best see which new ideas should be developed and tested in *their* area. The same person will *also* be the one who can best assess what will work as an improvement, and what will not work and thus should be discarded. This is information that most leaders (naturally enough) have no firsthand access to. If you lose the employees' commitment in this area, you lose a substantial resource for innovation in the enterprise.[15]

3. Naturally enough, in our context we have been focused on people's *reactions* to false participation. We have seen that broken expectations create irritation and resignation. But it is also important to not lose sight of the fact that false participation *also* leads to a weaker basis for making good decisions. The reason is simply that the decision-maker may overlook relevant knowledge. Genuine participation provides leaders with a wider scope of experience and insight, and they can therefore base their choices on this. This is clearly a better base for assessing what is the best way forward. This applies to minor as well as major details. Consider the example with the floor covering where it probably was not a good idea to buy the white surface. The workers who have to clean the floor will know that it will be difficult to maintain its presentability.

But what is most striking in this example is the experience of false participation. It did not matter what the cleaner said, even if she probably had the best argument. It is one thing to accept that others make poor decisions that become your problem, but it is *especially* painful when you find that the invitation to take part in the decision-making was just for show.

A Nordic meeting hell?

Most of the messages in this book have general validity. However, when it comes to participation it is necessary to keep in mind where we are in the world. We have pointed out how the distance between leader and employee is shorter in the Nordic countries than in many other parts of the world. This affects expectations but also provides opportunities. Here an Asian employee tells us about his encounter with his Norwegian leader:

> When our leader at the start came to us inviting us to come with our advice we did not understand what he meant. In my homeland leaders do not ask for advice. To us this is a sign of a weak leader. The leader is the one who must make decisions, that's the leader's job. I felt uncomfortable talking to him about this. I should give him advice? No, that was strange.[16]

Most employees in the Nordic countries would not react in this way if asked by their leader to give advice. Indeed the opposite is the case; they will typically assume they have influence in many contexts. This is reflected in legislation assigning both the right and obligation to take part in participation.[17] This obviously does not mean that employees can decide 'everything' that takes place in an organization. In the Nordic countries much power is still in the hands of the employer and the formal leaders. The false participation phenomenon does not mean that people should always have things the way they want. The problem rather appears to arise when the boundaries or *framework* for the participation is vague. Could the Nordic context or leadership style be a reason for this?

Let us look at an example from Norway. A recent leadership study discusses the advantages and disadvantages of the 'Norwegian leadership style.'[18] Among the upsides is the idea that the 'trial and error approach is permissible.' This is a clear positive feature in our context because innovation requires testing and tolerance, as failures can occur (see Chapter 4). Among the disadvantages of the Norwegian leadership style, you will find, on the other hand, the *amount* of participation. Specifically, this criticism refers to the number of meetings. The strong urge to involve workers may actually result in a 'Nordic meeting hell':

> Meetings that crawl ahead, apparently without goal, meaning or a clear agenda. Preferably dominated by individuals who have no basis for saying what they're saying. But they say it anyway.[19]

Some will certainly find this description all too familiar, probably mostly office workers. The most interesting point in the study is still this: that when meetings lack an agenda with a clear purpose and framework, the *real* decisions are moved out into the corridors. Informal meeting points (outside the meeting itself) then become the most important arenas for influence. Thus the intention of genuine participation will be undermined. Moreover, the road to experiencing false participation is a short one in such situations. Everyone is invited to speak out in the meetings, but the final decision is made according to completely different conversations.

Considering what should be done in a meeting therefore appears to be particularly important in the Nordic context. This becomes even more important when planning to introduce changes where the people involved feel that much is at stake. *Then frameworks should be defined for what you can have influence on and what is set in stone*. The reason is that these frameworks will affect the expectations that are created — both for the leaders and the co-workers. This will of course also apply to 'consultations,' committee work, and other types of participation measures.[20]

Thus a leader should clarify what can be discussed, and (when necessary) what is *not* open to debate. At times this may certainly lead to a meta-discussion of the frameworks involved. The main message in this chapter at any rate is that when you invite and involve co-workers to participate, you should truly and honestly mean it. And then it will also be easier to have a keener awareness of the possibilities and limitations of the participation, both for the leaders and the co-workers.

Balanced participation

Finally, I will return to a point from an earlier chapter. Many organizations are facing the following dilemma: The work on change and innovation must occur *together with* the normal daily operations. This applies both to organizations supplying public services and to enterprises competing in a market. In practice this means that it is difficult to dedicate *too much* effort on one or the other side of the dilemma: Focusing too much on the day-to-day operations makes it difficult to develop and try out new things, whereas too much focus on change and innovation will challenge the day-to-day operations.[21]

If change is to succeed, it will be necessary to put an effort into participation. This does not mean that *as much as possible* is always the best solution – even if it is well intended. Let us start with a specific example. Here a newly hired intermediate leader tells us about her encounter with an intense participation culture:

> Some weeks ago I received an email asking me to attend a meeting about a technical change. I just put it away, thinking that it had come to the wrong person, because I know zilch about such things. Not only that, it's also not within my area of responsibility or work, so I promptly forgot the whole thing. But you know what? After some days they called me and wondered why they hadn't heard from me and so on ... So I felt I had to attend this meeting.[22]

This informant does not see the point of being involved in this case. She has nothing to add to the case, and it has nothing to do with her as a leader. We can illuminate this example with a research approach that is somewhat critical of exaggerated use of participation. The idea is to look for a balance where employees *can participate at the level they want and expect*. This is called 'participation satisfaction.'[23]

Here 'satisfaction' is the ideal middle point on a scale with extremes at opposite ends. If you participate more than you want, you will be 'oversaturated.' If you want more participation than you are allowed, you get 'hungry.' Neither option is favorable, not for the individual or for the organization. This middle manager is in danger of being oversaturated in her new organization. In this case, the organization would probably also have been better served if she had used her energy on something other than the meeting in question.

Bearing this in mind, a fitting end to the chapter is to encourage leaders to use a degree of common sense. This may be reasonable in a book such as this, geared as it is towards innovation and change. Let us therefore listen to the following leader, who has had much experience in change work:

> Those leaders who join [an organization] believing that they will get everyone on board … I don't believe it, you don't have a chance, you can't get everyone to join. You need a critical mass which drives the change, and then you have to leave the others in peace, really. Let them work with their stuff, we also need this factory working from day to day.[24]

We will not discuss this strategy, nor talk about how optimistic change-leaders can allow themselves to be. But it is a good idea to think about the following: Those who are not always as enthusiastic about change (and participation) still have a vital task, namely to maintain quality in the day-to-day operations of their organization.

Chapter 8

Listening Leadership

Are you a good listener? According to a prominent psychiatrist the answer is probably 'no.' In a newspaper article he bluntly says that nobody is a particularly good listener. He also uses an original expression as the rationale for his answer: 'There are many forms of mental earplugs. Such as prejudices, arrogance, and overconfidence.'[1]

The fact that listening is difficult obviously does not make it less important, particularly for leaders. I must admit that my ears pricked up during an interview with the CEO of the gigantic Norwegian Oil Fund.[2] This successful financier chose to call 'listening leadership' his basic philosophy. My associations (or personal prejudices) relating to financial gurus go in a somewhat different direction. But this is the way he answers a question about what he is going to bring with him into his new job:

> I believe that you bring a heap of things into leadership. And at the bottom of it really — probably mostly — is listening, I think. I believe leaders need to be much better at listening.[3]

A leader who has had success in London's world of finance can hardly be called particularly soft and yielding. Thus we can put to rest the idea that a listening attitude makes a leader weak or unclear. The CEO of the Oil Fund states that he listens to 'make better decisions' and to 'make it easier to do things later.'

His rationale makes it clear that listening is not about abdicating his role of leader. The underlying thought is rather acknowledging that you are not smarter than everybody else —

even if you are their leader. Another Nordic leader who has come to the same realization is a former Norwegian Finance Minister and Minister of Education and Research. She is now head of a research institute. Her pragmatic attitude to leadership is quite down to earth:

> My advice is to set some goals but to be openminded when it comes to means to achieve them. Many people have something to contribute that you didn't think about yourself. And you can reach the goal you have if you listen to what others have to say.[4]

As this chapter proceeds, we will see that listening leadership is a reasonable strategy for having success with change and innovation. To examine this, we must consider what leadership is, but also look at some skills in dialogue and communication.

We will start with a dramatic story that sets the theme by way of contrast:[5]

Arrogance in Japanese

Early in the morning on 11 March 2011 there is a powerful earthquake off the east coast of Japan. Barely an hour later the waves roll across the walls of the Fukushima nuclear power station. Water floods the facility and ruins emergency power-generators and cooling pumps. Then meltdown starts in three of the reactors, followed by explosions in the main building. Radioactive substances have started to spread out into the environment. The worst nuclear disaster since Chernobyl is now a fact.

The earthquake which triggered it all was the most powerful ever registered in Japan. Together with the resultant tsunami, the quake caused unavoidable damage, killing more than 15,000 people. In spite of this, there is in the aftermath broad agreement that the Fukushima accident could have been avoided. Or to be blunter, it *should* have been avoided. The fact is that there was no lack of open warnings in the years preceding the accident. The criticism came from researchers and targeted directly how Japanese nuclear power stations were inadequately protected from earthquakes. Intense arguments from experts had been heard advising that the height of the protective wall around the Fukushima power station should be raised. All warnings and proposals were rejected by the authorities and the nuclear-power industry.

We will not look further into the details of this accident here. Neither will we delve into the consequences of the accident, but it is worth noting that the ripple effects were significant: Europe's energy security is still weakened due to the skepticism towards nuclear power triggered by Fukushima.[6]

Anyway, in our context, the point of telling this story is to illustrate an essential point: Allow me to look back at the chapter on fearlessness, which was about psychological safety. More specifically, it was about the advantage of having a climate where people dare to speak freely and openly without fear of consequences. This is a good basis for an organization which wants to reach its goals. However, and this is the point: It assumes that someone is listening. It is useless for people to be willing to share their knowledge if there is nobody there to deal actively with what is stated and shared.

In the Fukushima story there was indeed no lack of free utterances. The problem was the failure at the other end: None of the decision-makers listened to the input with interest and openness. The input was rather dismissed with an overconfidence or smugness that had major negative consequences. The authorities and the nuclear industry had a tight-knit and exclusive relationship in Japan. Knowledgeable researchers who had voiced warnings and proposed measures were considered 'outsiders.' They were called speculative and not worth being listened to.[7] With this type of mental earplugs it is difficult to listen and actually understand what is being said.

Creating results with the help of others

An often-used definition of leadership is that 'Leadership is about creating results with the help of others.' In fact, this phrase really cannot be called a definition as it only states something about what leadership *should lead to* (results), and not what it really is *in itself*.[8] However, something essential emerges in this familiar saying. Leadership is something that arises and is performed *between* people; in other words, it is a relational phenomenon. Or to put it in another, somewhat banal, way: A leader without someone to lead is not a leader.[9]

Is it possible to state something all-encompassing about what you should *be able to do* as a leader? To start with, the question is unsettlingly demanding for an organization researcher (in this case me), even if answers to this question have been proposed. On an overarching level, leader competence can be divided into three types.[10]

First, a type of administrative competence is required. The day-to-day business must function in practice. A good picture of this can be made by describing leadership as a mix of poetry and plumbing. In other words: There is no point in having grand views of roads to take, and meaning to give to an organization, if the toilets do not work.[11]

Second, technical competence is required. This means that you have some understanding of the area you are to lead. You do not need to be a 'complete expert' in a given trade to function as a leader. At the same time, it is not enough to be a 'purely professional' leader — a person who does not know *anything* about what the organization does or produces.

I hasten to add that there are different traditions relating to this. A study of leaders in the UK and Germany can serve as an example of two different leadership ideals. German middle managers have a lot of competence in the field; for example, they *themselves* are capable of solving technical problems. The ideal of having strong technical competence is rather important in Germany. In the UK, on the other hand, the ideal of the professional leader is stronger, which means that leadership is considered to be more of a profession in itself. To put it in black and white: The British middle manager can probably not contribute to solving a technical problem but will instead assemble a group of specialists to deal with the case.[12]

It is fair to say that 'Nordic leadership,' for example, can be placed somewhere between the ideals of a professional versus a technical leadership. But there are also variations based on contexts and the people in question. The discussion about these two ideals will continue, not only in the Nordic countries. Part of this is related to the question of *how much* technical knowledge one needs to have. What is enough? The two leaders presented at the start of this chapter differ in that one heads a fund based on his background as an economist (among other things), while the other one leads researchers without having a researcher background.

This brings us to the *third* type of competence a leader should have. This deals with 'getting the organization to succeed in practice.'[13] This may simply be called (somewhat mystically) 'leadership competence.'

In research, we can approach this by highlighting the specific link between *personality traits* and so-called 'effective leadership.' Seen in this way, leaders who succeed in their job have *some* tendency to be:[14]

- Extroverted — they enjoy communicating with others
- Friendly and collaboration-oriented
- Open to experiences and curious
- Emotionally stable
- Conscientious

This must not be understood as a recipe for success. Critics will even claim that emphasizing leadership qualities represents an unfortunate personality-focus (and an exaggerated attention on leaders) in the research. Above, we suggested that leadership occurs in *interaction* between leaders and co-workers. Some researchers turn this around by asking whether perhaps leaders are only as effective and successful as their employees allow them to be.[15]

Obviously we do not need to consider the traits listed above as the template. It rather helps us to see trends and patterns that can offer *some* information about suitable leadership qualities. The first three points agree with the ideal of a *listening leadership*: An interest in collaboration and a desire to communicate serves well as a proactive starting point. It becomes even clearer in the third point: Openness and curiosity are important ingredients in a genuine listening attitude.

Bearing all this in mind, listening as a practice will now be examined in more detail. How is one a good listener, and what is required to practice good listening leadership?

Listening to understand others

I started this chapter by suggesting that most of us are not very good listeners at all. Here one leader talks about his listening practice:

> I love talking. I also suspect that I listen most to hear what I myself can say. I have to admit that. This can of course be called a negative trait, because when I hear someone

> talking I quite quickly start to work out what I'm going to say. Because I'm ... I really want to say something.[16]

This leader is refreshingly honest in his description. He is most interested in communicating his views when with others. Input from others is primarily used as raw material for polishing his own opinions and message. The goal is to inform (or persuade) the other party about his own ideas. It will not be surprising if you recognize some of yourself in this.[17]

The downside of such a one-way model of communication is glaring: You will not get a firm grip on the other party's knowledge and perspectives. A more *dialogic* communication form would allow you to exploit the experience and knowledge resources in your organization much better. This requires that you strike a balance between offering your personal views and inquisitively exploring those of others. Let us consider what characterizes such communication.[18]

Dialogic communication is based on the following attitudes, actions, or abilities:

1. You assume that others have something to teach you.
2. You explore the viewpoints of others.
3. You express yourself but avoid devaluing others.
4. You build on the views of others when you construct your own.
5. You are able to adopt the perspectives of others.

The first point is about assuming a learning attitude. Your starting point is that others may have seen or understood something you have not discovered yet. The existence of differences between people (diversity) provides a clear advantage here, because it increases the opportunity to learn something.

The second point is about trying to understand the views of others, *even* if you disagree or do not initially understand them. The point is to be curious and explore the *grounds* behind a point of view: Which premises and rationales have led to this? Which logical thinking has led to this (strange) position? The essence here is to adopt a listening attitude to the other party:

> Listening is about allowing your own idea to rest for a while and really concentrate on what the other person is saying. When we listen we follow the rationales and explore them through questions if there is something we do not understand. This enables us to understand according to their premises.[19]

Listening, then, does not actually mean being silent in a literal sense but being willing to explore. Here we can distinguish between two ways of listening.[20] While *inner listening* is directed towards ourselves, *focused listening* is directed towards the person we are listening to. With inner listening, we start from our own experience. As soon as we hear something from the other person, we begin to search in our own 'inner archive' for recognition (like the leader above). Thus, we understand what is being said from our own perspective. This is a familiar situation, but we don't expand our knowledge of the other person's perspective much this way. The purpose of focused listening, on the other hand, is to find out what makes sense *for the person you are listening to*. This requires you to listen with a more open, curious, and exploratory attitude. For most of us, it is a bit challenging to shift from inner listening to focused listening. The payoff, however, is that you will understand much more about what is happening around you.

The third point reminds us that the 'contract' in a real dialogue is a two-way street. Listening is necessary, but not sufficient. Dialogue requires that there is someone to listen to, 'something' to explore. The interlocutors must offer their opinions by trying to formulate their thoughts clearly and truthfully. But it is beneficial to remember here: Dialogue is impaired if it turns into a competition, where what is uttered is taken as disparaging the points of view of others. In that case, most of the interlocutors who are trying to explain themselves will lose the will to continue the dialogue.

The two final points on the list also make some demands on interlocutors. Item 4 is about trying to integrate the views of others into your own. When you build on other people's views, the possibility of developing something new increases (a new solution, a new position). The goal is that something else should occur other than your desire to win the discussion. That would only leave you with the point of view you already had before entering the dialogue. Which of course might be fair enough. The point is that it is never a good idea to start a *dialogue* where the goal is to win it.

The fifth and final point is about the ability to adopt the perspective of others in a certain situation. If this is to happen, you will have to put your feelings of superiority and your overconfidence and arrogance aside. The Fukushima nuclear power-plant accident could probably have been avoided if the decision-makers had been less misguided in their beliefs. They were not capable of envisioning any other scenarios than what had already been established.

Listening to solve problems

In reality it is not always easy to satisfy the five requirements in the list above. For example, it is difficult to adhere to such ideals when the communication is heated and a conflict situation is looming. The possibility of conflict is part of everyday life in organizations. Differences between individuals, functions, and entities can be a source of disagreement on how to solve problems. Occasionally, this may end in deadlocked conflicts.

Bearing this in mind, we will look here at a simple (but well-tried) approach to solving conflicts: a so-called *interest-based process*.[21]

The essence of this type of process is to distinguish between 'position' and 'interest.' These two words are used in a slightly different way than we are accustomed to but can be explained as follows. A 'position' comprises a specific solution to a problem. 'Interests' refer to what *underlies* and gives grounds for a position. It is reasonable to assume that there are some underlying needs and assessments that led you to adopt the position you have.

Let me use an example to illustrate the process. A college has two campuses, one large and one small. They lie in two separate municipalities, both with their own local IT service. Through recent mergers, the number of academic employees has increased substantially. This means the IT service's workload has exploded. This is a problem that has not been solved.

We can imagine that there are two different solutions to the problem, that is, two 'positions':

A. Make the IT service more effective by assembling (and co-locating) all of it at the largest campus.
B. Keep the two sites that exist today, but increase staffing.

The organizational director at the college is in position A, while the employees (who would need to move) are in position B. In such a situation the standpoints may become uncompromising. The director is convinced about her solution, but the people affected by it are becoming more and more concerned. Everybody knows that the director has the power to win. Now the plan could be forced through, or it could be illuminated through an 'interest-based process.' How should they implement this? Four pieces of advice apply if they are to succeed in such a process:

1. Avoid confrontation; separate the people from the problem.
2. Ask the parties to *give rationales* for their position by explaining their assessments and needs.
3. Look for common interests.
4. Agree on how to solve the case.

On the first point: Accusations that the employees are stubborn and are simply rejecting change will raise the temperature. On the other hand, it is not helpful to hint, for example, that the director is incompetent at her job. The second point is the essence of the process. We can imagine a meeting being held, attended by both sides in the conflict. The meeting reveals essential information for everyone:

- The director believes that co-localization will strengthen the professional IT service in total. She explains that she envisions higher efficiency by allocating more resources to virtual online support. It has also become clear that the college does not have the money to hire more IT staff. But her primary interest is that all college employees will have better and faster IT support.
- The employees concerned believe that both IT services are strong enough. They describe a situation where some of the college's academic employees have very poor IT competence – and that they therefore need support from a person 'in the flesh.' Under the proposed solution, the IT staff will have to spend too much time on commuting to and from the smallest campus. Giving support is meaningful, but they would like to respond more quickly when people ask for help.

Both parties have now learned something they were not previously fully aware of. The employees realize that the financial parameters are fixed. Hiring more staff is thus not a viable solution. The director realizes that her purely online solution underestimates the need for physical presence (and that traveling would steal the IT staff's time).

The two parties also realize that they have a *common interest* in wanting the IT support to function better (point 3). The employees agree that the director has the power to decide, while she agrees to revise her solution – based on what has emerged (point 4). The new solution will be that half of the employees will move to the large new campus to work online, fulltime. The rest will remain to ensure support for those who need someone to come to them in person. The compromise may be somewhat 'gray and boring,' but it is the best solution in the present situation.

Listening to the rationales *underlying* a position turns out to be useful for both the leaders and the employees. This can be called 'double listening.'[22] The duality involves listening to people's protests or complaints while simultaneously seeking out the *underlying* sources of frustration. When the sources of a person's engagement come to light, the situation becomes easier to understand and work with. It is easy to imagine such a practice being used across a wide range of scenarios, from assuaging minor irritations about unclear lines of responsibility for two co-workers, to peace negotiations when the situation has become deadlocked.

Not least, listening can provide valuable insight for leaders making change initiatives. This could apply, for example, to the case above, where a limited and concrete plan is revised and improved. It can also be relevant to listen for response and 'reception' in an organization if larger and more complex change processes are implemented. At times, it may in fact be reasonable to adjust, revise, and (even) cancel ideas and plans for change.[23]

Finally in this chapter we will see that listening leadership also has an essential function when it comes to innovation work.

Listening for ideas

In a hospital the following idea is floated: What if each patient is issued with a pair of noise-canceling headsets? The hospital has four patients per ward. That makes it difficult to comply with confidentiality rules during the doctor's visit to the ward (even if the doctor lowers their voice when speaking with a patient). The dialogue between patient and doctor therefore takes place in poor conditions. The hospital managers have considered restructuring their building, and they have thought about moving the patient into the corridor. The headset idea will solve the problem. When the doctor talks with a patient, the three others put on their headset (with radio). Then the doctor and the patient can talk in confidence and the others will not hear what is being said.

This may be a modest innovation, but it is important enough for those concerned. We will examine what might be required for this innovation to be realized:

- Let us say that you are a doctor making your daily rounds in the ward in question. Being close to the problem, you have a *particularly favorable position* for finding good solutions. This is an advantage all practicians will have when it comes to innovation.
- Then the idea must come to you. Perhaps a colleague recently bought such a headset, and the idea hits you when she tells you about her new purchase — immediately after you have struggled with whispering to a patient.
- The next requirement is that you must deem it to be relevant (and feasible) to promote such an idea. It will be useful if you work in a place where looking for

improvement and development is common and seen as part of the job.

- Next, you need to have someone to go to with the idea. This should preferably be someone with power and resources, who therefore (possibly) can realize the idea. The role of leader is important here. In this specific case, funding is needed to purchase the headsets, and support will be needed for testing them. In this case the idea can come to fruition. At other times an idea will clash with parameters and other considerations, and the leader will then be unwilling to pursue the matter further. Most employees accept that. The point is, at any rate, that leaders must adopt a listening position and function as possible recipients if the idea is to come to fruition.

In innovation research, the process of acting as an agent for your idea, of employees working to gain acceptance in the organization, is often called 'championing.'[24] This concept has become more relevant as 'ordinary employees' have come to be recognized as significant sources of innovation for an organization. This applies to the private, public, and voluntary sectors.

Here the employee role is *expanded* from being simply a worker to being a participant in development. The employee is no longer the person who carries out the ideas that come from *other sources* (leaders or experts in house or externally). She or he becomes a source of innovation. This point will become even more central, as the use of artificial intelligence among certain groups of employees is strongly increasing. With these powerful tools, workers in various sectors will enhance their ability to create innovative solutions that the company can greatly benefit from — if the ideas are captured.

The person who is an agent for their idea will work to justify and explain it, for example by illustrating why the idea will be beneficial for the organization. Here the leader's role is to welcome and listen to the agent, and, if relevant, to use their authority or resources on the case. This of course does not mean that all ideas will or should be realized. But there should be one or another form of proactive listening. If not, the source of ideas will eventually dry up.[25]

Access to leaders with decision-making power and resources may obviously be perceived as somewhat limited for an employee, particularly in large organizations. Employees' immediate superiors, also close to practice, will therefore have key roles in listening, capturing, and promoting ideas from the practicians.[26]

All in all, the message in this chapter is that a listening leadership strengthens the organization's ability to change and innovate. We have seen that the ability to listen has clear advantages, but that listening may also be difficult to do. Perhaps you, the person reading this, are an excellent listener. At any rate, it is tempting to conclude with the general challenge from the start of this chapter: Leaders must be much better at listening.

Afterword: Something to Reach For Together

The idea of this book about a dream organization for change and innovation resulted in the following model:

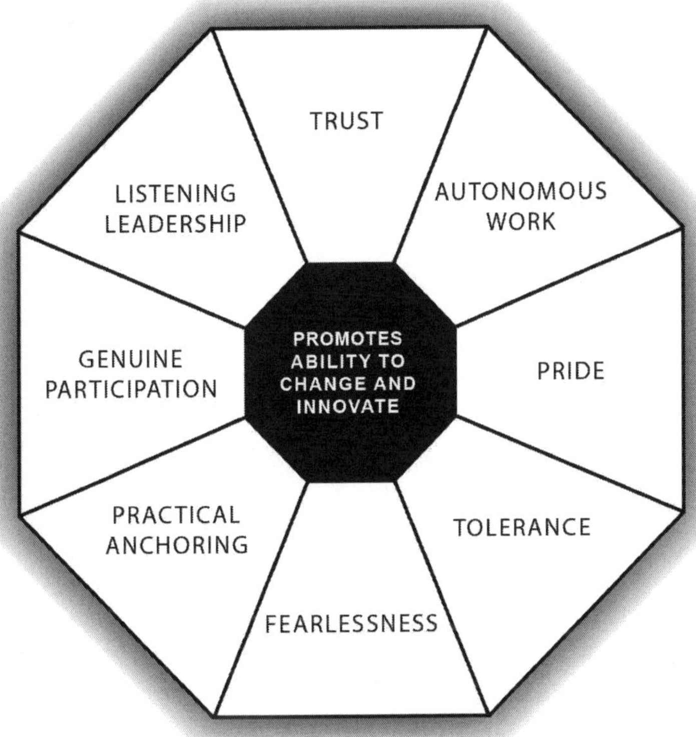

The Diamond Model for Change and Innovation

The purpose of the eight preceding chapters has been to explain *why* and *how* these features strengthen the ability to change and innovate in organizations. Summing up, I have described an *idealized* organization. This is a point worth noting: The description of the dream organization should not lead to paralysis of the type, 'We'll never reach this ideal, so we might as well give up right now.'

It is more constructive to think of an idealization as a vision or *goal picture* — a useful idea about *where we would like to be*. Let us listen to a philosopher who believes we should be better at raising our sights a little, and that we generally fall short when it comes to formulating ideas. He uses an analogy about a car trip to explain his view:

> Say that we're driving in a large car together. Then it would be very odd to only think about where we are on the road just now and which way to go at the next junction. We should also have an idea about which city we're going to — in the longer term. Where are we trying to get to? I would have liked to see that we dared to be more utopian in this sense. At the same time, we don't need to believe that it's easy to get there. Because it's obviously terribly difficult to achieve something ideal. But while it could be very difficult, it would be very good if we managed to do it.[1]

Working on *goals* is a key task for leaders; this give the organization a direction. This does not only concern the specific goals for the organization, but also more long-term goals and visions for *how the organization itself should appear*. Using this perspective, this book is interesting for leaders, particularly leaders who would like to build and improve their organization's ability to change and innovate. For many organizations, these improvements will make it easier to satisfy the true purpose of the enterprise. Change and innovation are not goals in themselves. The point is to improve the ability to realize goals.

In the introductory chapter, I asked you to (while reading) think about and 'adapt' the content of the book to make it optimally relevant for your own organization. In this way, you can create a concrete and realistic 'recipe' for what needs to be done next. Parts of this book are easily adaptable, while other parts require such questions as: What would this correspond to in our organization? What does this mean to us? How can we work to achieve this? Of course, it will be necessary to involve and engage colleagues to achieve a common understanding of the challenges and the steps you want to take.

If you are a leader, you have a special responsibility in this work. Use the phenomenon of trust as an example (at the top of the model). Trust does not stand on its own and does not simply spring into being in an organization. Trust can establish itself if supported by power. As a leader, you can apply your power to influence the organization in all the eight areas in the model above, some more directly than others.

And then, of course, I must immediately add that a leader cannot accomplish much if the employee 'on the floor' does not take on his or her part of the responsibility for implementing change. Collaboration between leaders and employees is necessary to develop the organization in the direction the book outlines.

Acknowledgments

This book has been made possible thanks to a research term granted and funded by my employer, the Norwegian University of Science and Technology. The people around me have of course also been important. My wife, Monica Seland, has been my clearheaded 'in house' reader, with her experience from research, writing, and leadership in practice.

Thanks are also due to my colleagues at my daily workplace in the Department of Education and Lifelong Learning. Some of them have been helpful through the seminars in the research group COOL (Conditions for Learning and Innovation in Higher Education and Work), and others through more 'random' but valuable academic and social encounters. I am also pleased to have had the opportunity to participate in the management group in my department for some years. To work with experienced and smart leaders like this was both educational and inspiring for an organizational researcher.

Next, I would like to thank my longstanding publisher, Gyldendal Akademisk, represented by editor Knut André Karlstad, who has been a steady and excellent collaborator for me as an author. I appreciate that they also were positive about the creation of this book.

Although this book is quite short, it represents a rather long academic journey. Down through the years, I have been part of various expert environments, networks, and research projects. This has given me the opportunity to discuss and collaborate with many skilled professionals, both in and outside the university. In terms of the specific themes in this book, my long-lasting collaboration with Tone Merethe Aasen and Trond Kongsvik has been particularly important. In addition, I would like to acknowledge the experts who have read and thus contributed to the peer review of the manuscript for this book. This role is anonymous, but no less significant.

Finally, it's important not to forget that researchers like me also rely on organizations to make themselves available for research. Therefore, I would like to express my gratitude to all the leaders and employees who have been willing to share their knowledge and experience with me in different projects.

Notes

For your information: To find the source being referenced, you use the surname provided in the note. Based on this name, you will find the full reference in the alphabetical list of sources at the back of the book.

Preface

1 Adapted from Conan Doyle, A. (1890/2014).
2 Kvadsheim, S. (2021); Pletten, C. (2021).

Introduction

1 Norwegian University of Science and Technology (2023).
2 Karlsen, J.E. (2015), p. 23.
3 Maslow, A.H. (1968).
4 For example, Kværner, K. (2020).
5 Bøhn, E.D. (2019), p. 125.
6 For example, Woodward, S. & Hendry, C. (2004); Karp, T. & Helgø, T.I. (2008); Parker, D. & Grandy, G. (2009).
7 Cf. Amundsen, O., Amble, N., & Rismark, M. (2020).
8 Bolman, L.G. & Deal, T.E. (2017), p. 7.
9 Adapted from Geissler, H. (2018), p. 51 (my translation).
10 Kellermann, B. (2004).
11 Von Oettingen, A. & Mellon, K. (eds) (2020), p. 55. *[Pissedårlig ledelse]*

Chapter 1: Trust

1 Bævre, A.I. (2019) (my translation).
2 Adapted from Brandi, U. & Hasse, C. (2012).
3 Julsrud, T.E. (2018).
4 Julsrud, T.E. (2018).
5 Bringselius, L. (2021); Mayer, R.C., Davis, J.H., & Schoorman, D.F. (1995).

6 Grimen, H. (2009).

7 Sørhaug, T. (1996).

8 Sørhaug, T. (1996), p. 54.

9 Sørhaug, T. (1996), p. 22.

10 Amundsen, O. (2014); Amundsen, O. & Kongsvik, T. (2016).

11 Adapted from Amundsen, O. & Kongsvik, T. (2016), p. 65.

12 Ahmed, P.K. (1998); Van de Ven, A.H., Polley, D.E., Garud, R., & Venkataraman, S. (1999); Hansen, K., Amundsen, O., Aasen, T.M., & Gressgård, L.J. (2017).

13 For example, Sitkin, S.B. & Stickel, D. (1996); Julsrud, T.E. (2018).

14 McLean, L.D. (2005); Kuvaas, B. & Dysvik, A. (2020).

15 Adapted from Nørmark, D. & Fogh Jensen, A. (2021), p. 222.

16 Storey, J. & Salaman, G. (2005; 2009).

17 Bringselius, L. (2021).

18 Rotenberg, K.J. (2018); Cohen-Charash, Y. & Spector, P.E. (2001).

19 Glasø, L. & Martinsen, Ø.L. (2018).

Chapter 2: Autonomous Work

1 Amabile, T.M. (1988); De Jong, J.P.J. & Kemp, R. (2003); McLean, L.D. (2005); Smith, P., Kesting, P., & Ulhøi, J.P. (2008); Jain, A., Dedieu, V., Zwetsloot, G., & Leka, S. (2017).

2 Hilland, J. & Kjerpeseth, J.E. (2019).

3 Alvesson, M. & Spicer, A. (2016).

4 Alvesson, M. & Spicer, A. (2016), p. 127 (my translation).

5 Bonvik, Ø. (2015). *[Frist meg ikke inn i lederskap]*

6 Bonvik, Ø., Lorentz, C., & Martinsen, Ø. (2019).

7 Foss, N.J. & Klein, P.G. (2022).

8 Deci, E.L. & Ryan, R.M. (1985); Ryan, R.M. & Deci, E.L. (2017).

9 Olafsen, A.H. (2018).

10 McGregor, D. (1960).
11 Kaspersen, L. (2010).
12 Kuvaas, B. (ed.) (2008).
13 Wilhelmsen, P.N. (2018).
14 Kuvaas, B. & Dysvik, A. (2020), p. 57.
15 Kuvaas, B. (ed.) (2008); Kuvaas, B. & Dysvik, A. (2020).
16 Kaspersen, L. (2013).
17 Deci, E.L., Koestner, R., & Ryan, R.M. (1999); Frey, B.S. & Jegen, R. (2001); Kvalnes, Ø. (2020).
18 Olafsen, A.H. (2018).
19 Ryan, R.M. & Deci, E.L. (2017); Olafsen, A.H. (2018).
20 Foss, N.J., Minbaeva, D.B., Pedersen, T., & Reinholt, M. (2009); Hon, A.H.Y. (2012); Ryan, R.M. & Deci, E.L. (2017); Olafsen, A.H. (2018).
21 Aasen, T.M. & Amundsen, O. (2011).
22 Glasø, L. & Martinsen, Ø.L. (2018); Amundsen, S. & Martinsen, Ø.L. (2014).

Chapter 3: Pride

1 Fineman, S. (2000); Kaufmann, G. & Kaufmann, A. (2009/2015).
2 *The New Oxford Dictionary of English* (1989).
3 Guddal, R. (2019).
4 Grann, I. (2019).
5 Aasen, T.M., Amundsen, O., Gressgård, L.J., & Hansen, K. (2012); Amundsen, O., Aasen, T.M., Gressgård, L.J., & Hansen, K. (2014); Gressgård, L.J., Amundsen, O., Aasen, T.M., & Hansen, K. (2014).
6 Lyubomirsky, S., King, L., & Diener, E. (2005); Kaufmann, G. & Kaufmann, A. (2009/2015).
7 Adapted from Svendsen, L.F.H. (2015), p. 43.
8 Adapted from Graeber, D. (2018), p. 45.
9 Prilleltensky, I. (2020).
10 Paradisi, M., Matera, C., & Nerini, A. (2024).

11 Porter, L.W., Steers, R.M., Mowday, R.T., & Boulian, P.V. (1974); Payne, S.C. & Huffman, A.H. (2005).
12 Sinek, S. (2009); Sinek, S. (2017).
13 Glorvigen, M. (2019); Hollensbe, E., Wookeey, C., Hickey, L., & George, G. (2014).
14 Meyer, J.W. & Allen, N.J. (1997); Knippenberg, D. & Sleebos, E. (2006).
15 For example, Blyton, P. & Jenkins, J. (2007).
16 Rotenberg, K.J. (2018).
17 Seligman, M.E.P. & Schulman, P. (1986); Baas, M., De Dreu, C.K.W., & Nijstad, B.A. (2008); Kaufmann, G. & Kaufmann, A. (2009/2015).
18 George, J.M. (2000); Fredrickson, B.L. (2001); Spector, P.E. & Fox, S. (2010); Kaufmann, G. & Kaufmann, A. (2009/2015).
19 Van Scotter, J.R. & Motowidlo, S.J. (1996).
20 Barnett, M., Jermier, J., & Lafferty, B. (2006).
21 Brønn, P.S. (2020).
22 Thomas, W.I. & Thomas, D.S. (1928), in Tjora, A. (2018).

Chapter 4: Tolerance

1 Garborg, R. & Kjerpeseth, J.E. (2019).
2 Brenna, L.R. (2018), p. 49.
3 Alvesson, M. & Spicer, A. (2016).
4 Thomas, D.A. & Ely, R.J. (1996); Brenna, L.R. (2018).
5 Horwitz, S.K. & Horwitz, I.B. (2007); Bang, H. & Midelfart, T.N. (2019).
6 Hülsheger, U.R., Anderson, N., & Salgado, J.F. (2009); Oddane, T. (2017).
7 Høgh-Olesen, H. (1995).
8 Schiefloe, P.M. (2003).
9 Schiefloe, P.M. (2003), p. 316.
10 Eilertsen, T. & Glomnes, L. (2020).
11 Oddane, T. (2017).
12 Eggen, N.A. (1999/2016), p. 225.

13 Ahmed, P.K. (1998); Aasen, T.M. & Amundsen, O. (2015), p. 153.
14 Lysklett, S.R. (2007), p. 262.
15 Michie, S.G., Dooley, R.S., & Fryxell, G.E. (2002); Bang, H. & Midelfart, T.N. (2019).
16 Cannella, A.A., Park, J.H., & Lee, H.U. (2008); Bang, H. & Midelfart, T.N. (2019).
17 Ahmed, P.K. (1998); Aasen, T.M. & Amundsen, O. (2015), p. 152.
18 Muller, J.Z. (2018).
19 Edmondson, A. (2023).
20 Le Coze, J.C. (2015).
21 Milch, V. & Laumann, K. (2016).

Chapter 5: Fearlessness

1 Breivik, M. & Larsen, V. (2020).
2 For example, Hemmestad, L.B. (2013).
3 Adapted from Edmondson, A. (2019).
4 O'Donoghue, T. & Rabin, M. (1999); Delaney, L. & Lades, L. (2017).
5 Newman, D.M. (1995).
6 Adapted from Edmondson, A. (2019), p. xvi.
7 Edmondson, A. (2019).
8 Edmondson, A. (2019).
9 Baer, M. & Frese, M. (2003); Frese, M. & Keith, N. (2015); Edmondson, A. (2019).
10 Amble, N., Amundsen, O., & Rismark, M. (eds) (2020).
11 Amundsen, O. & Rismark, M. (2020).
12 Fyhn, B. (2023).
13 Aasen, T.M. & Amundsen, O. (2011); Høyrup, S. (2020).
14 Darsø, L. (2011); Høyrup, S. (2020); Johansen, T., Specht, T., & Kleive, H. (2020).
15 Darsø, L. (2011).
16 Rismark, M. & Amundsen, O. (2020).
17 Adapted from Edmondson, A. (2019), p. 203.
18 Trulsen, O.N. (2011).

Chapter 6: Practical Anchoring

1 Karp, T. & Helgø, T.I. (2008); Parker, D. & Grandy, G. (2009); Aagestad, C., Tynes, T., Sterud, T., Johannessen, H.A., Gravseth, H.M., Løvseth, E.K., Alfonso, J.H., & Aasnæss, S. (2015).
2 'Change in Organizations'; cf. Amundsen, O. & Kongsvik, T. (2008/2016); Amundsen, O., Kongsvik, T., Olsen, H.H., & Munkvold, G. (2013).
3 Meyer, C.B. & Stensaker, I.G. (2011).
4 Adapted from Sjøvold, E. (2016).
5 Alvesson, M. & Svenningsson, S. (2008).
6 Amundsen, O. & Kongsvik, T. (2008/2016).
7 Ørsted, C. (2020), p. 211 [*Fatale forandringer*].
8 Scott, C.D. & Jaffe, D.T. (2004); Erwin, D.G. & Garman, A.N. (2010).
9 Scott, C.D. & Jaffe, D.T. (2004).
10 Bupp, N. (1996); Elrod, P.D. & Tippett, D.D. (2002).
11 Ørsted, C. (2020).
12 Thomas, R. & Hardy, C. (2011); Alvesson, M. & Svenningsson, S. (2014).
13 Ford, J.D. & Ford, L.W. (2009).
14 Adapted from Jacobsen, D.I. (2018).
15 Kvaal, I. (2014).
16 Brinkmann, S. (2019).
17 Hennestad, B.W. & Revang, Ø. (2017); Hamel, G. & Zanini, M. (2020).
18 Cf. for example Klev, R. & Levin, M. (2012).

Chapter 7: Genuine Participation

1 Giertsen, T. & Giæver, A. (2020).
2 Mustosmaki, A. (2017); Sergui, P.I., Şorcaru, S.L., Panaitescu, M., & Prunău, N.F. (2023).
3 Preuss, B. (2017); Levin, M., Nilssen, T., Ravn, J.E., & Øyum, L. (2012).

4 Wilkinson, A., Gollan, P.J., Marchington, M., & Lewin, D. (2010); Pot, F. (2017); Klev, R. & Levin, M. (2012).
5 Norvik, H. & Kjerpeseth, J.E. (2019).
6 Kongsvik, T.Ø. (2006), pp. 168–95.
7 From Gjøsund, G. (2009), pp. 102–3.
8 Stensaker, I. & Haueng, A.C. (2016), p. 75.
9 Levin, M. & Klev, R. (2002); Amundsen, O. & Kongsvik, T. (2008/2016).
10 Wilkinson, A., Gollan, P.J., Marchington, M., & Lewin, D. (eds) (2010).
11 Meyer, C.B. & Stensaker, I.G. (2011), p. 17.
12 Amundsen, O. (2014); Amundsen, O. & Kongsvik, T. (2008/2016).
13 Stensaker, I., Meyer, C.B., Falkenberg, J., & Haueng, A.C. (2001).
14 Amabile, T.M. (1988).
15 Høyrup, S., Bonnafous-Boucher, M., Hasse, C., Lotz, M., & Møller, K. (eds) (2012).
16 Sund, B. (2019), p. 62.
17 AML (2005); Vanebo, J.O. (2016).
18 Sund, B. (2019).
19 Sund, B. (2019), p. 91.
20 Amundsen, O., Kongsvik, T., Olsen, H.H., & Munkvold, G. (2013); Vestergaard, B. (2012).
21 Ettlie, J.E. (2006); Tidd, J. & Bessant, J. (2009).
22 Amundsen, O. (2003), p. 208.
23 Irgens, E.J. (2011).
24 Traaseth, A.K., Brenna, N. & Eia, H. (2020).

Chapter 8: Listening Leadership

1 Skårderud, F. (2020).
2 Its formal name is: The Norwegian Government Pension Fund Global (value on 26.03.2024: $1,624,483,000,000).
3 Tangen, N., Jones, M., & Sverdrup, T. (2021).

4 Halvorsen, K. & Apeland, O.C. (2020).
5 Edmondson, A. (2019); Hofstad, K. & Rosvold, K.A. (2021).
6 Harvey, F, Vidal, J., & Carrington, D. (2012).
7 Fackler, M. (2012).
8 Arnulf, J.K. (2021), p. 15.
9 Svenningson, S. & Alvesson, M. (2016), p. 106.
10 Arnulf, J.K. (2021); Vanebo, J.O. (2016).
11 Jacobsen, D.I. & Thorsvik, J. (2019).
12 Vie, O.E. (2012).
13 Arnulf, J.K. (2021), p. 97.
14 Arnulf, J.K. (2021).
15 Svenningson, S. & Alvesson, M. (2016), p. 15.
16 Adapted from Storeide, K. (2013), p. 36.
17 Clampitt, P.G. (2013).
18 Adapted from Bang, H. & Midelfart, T.N. (2019) and Isaacs, W. (1999).
19 Nygårdsvik, I. (unpublished) [in Bang, H. & Midelfart, T.N. (2019), p. 137].
20 Fikse, C. (2020).
21 Martin, A. (2021).
22 Fikse, C. (2020).
23 Alvesson, M. & Svenningson, S. (2008).
24 Lempiälä, T., Kauhaluoma, S.Y., & Näsänen, J. (2018); Høyrup, S. (2020).
25 Klitmøller, A., Lauring, J., & Christensen, P.R. (2007).
26 Hansen, K., Amundsen, O., Aasen, T.M., & Gressgård, L.J. (2017).

Afterword: Something to Reach For Together

1 Adapted from Moen, O.M. & Myrtveit, A.C. (2020).

Literature and references

Ahmed, P.K. (1998) 'Culture and climate for innovation.' *European Journal of Innovation Management*, Vol. 1, No. 1, pp. 30–43.

Alvesson, M. & Spicer, A. (2016) *Stupidity Paradox. The Power and Pitfalls of Functional Stupidity at Work*. London: Profile Books.

Alvesson, M. & Svenningson, S. (2008) *Changing Organizational Culture. Cultural Change Work in Progress*. London: Routledge.

Alvesson, M. & Svenningson, S. (2014) *Förändringsarbete i organisationer [Change in Organizations]*. Stockholm: Liber.

Amabile, T.M. (1988) 'A model of creativity and innovation in organizations.' *Research in Organizational Behavior*, Vol. 10, pp. 123–67.

Amble, N., Amundsen, O., & Rismark, M. (eds) (2020) *Medarbeiderdrevet innovasjon [Employee-Driven Innovation]*. Oslo: Gyldendal Akademisk.

AML (2005) *Arbeidsmiljøloven [The Working Environment Act]*.

Amundsen, O. (2003) *Fortellinger om forandring. En narrativ studie av planlagt organisasjonsendringi et norsk finanskonsern [Stories about change. A narrative study on planned organizational change in a Norwegian financial group*]. PhD thesis, Norwegian University of Science and Technology.

Amundsen, O. (2014) 'Stories and scripts as "cultural constraints" in organisations.' *International Journal of Learning and Change*, Vol. 7, No. 3/4, pp. 197–210.

Amundsen, O., Aasen, T.M., Gressgård, L.J., & Hansen, K. (2014) 'Preparing organisations for employee-driven open innovation.' *International Journal of Business Science and Applied Management*, Vol. 9, No. 1, pp. 24–35.

Amundsen, O., Amble, N., & Rismark, M. (2020) 'Innovasjon som fenomen og praksis' [Innovation as a phenomenon and practice], in Amble, N., Amundsen, O., & Rismark, M. (eds)

Medarbeiderdrevet innovasjon [Employee-Driven Innovation]. Oslo: Gyldendal Akademisk.

Amundsen, O. & Kongsvik, T. (2008/2016) *Endringskynisme. Og kunsten å skape god endringspraksis [Change Cynicism. And the Art of Creating Change]*. Oslo: Gyldendal Akademisk.

Amundsen, O., Kongsvik, T., Olsen, H.H., & Munkvold, G. (2013) 'Kriterier for gjennomføring av planlagte endringsprosesser: En eksplorerende casestudie' [Criteria for implementing planned change processes: An exploratory case study]. *Nordic Organization Studies*, Vol. 15, No. 1, pp. 3–28.

Amundsen, O., Aasen, T.M., Gressgård, L.J., & Hansen, K. (2014) 'Preparing organisations for employee-driven open innovation.' *International Journal of Business Science and Applied Management*, Vol. 9, No. 1, pp. 24–35.

Amundsen, O. & Rismark, M. (2020) 'Økt innovasjonskapasitet gjennom kulturell endring' [Increased innovation capacity through cultural change], in Amble, N., Amundsen, O., & Rismark, M. (eds) *Medarbeiderdrevet innovasjon [Employee-Driven Innovation]*. Oslo: Gyldendal Akademisk.

Amundsen, S. & Martinsen, Ø.L. (2014) 'Self-Other Agreement in Empowering Leadership: Relationships with Leader Effectiveness and Subordinates' Job Satisfaction and Turnover Intention.' *Leadership Quarterly*, Vol. 25, pp. 784–800.

Arnulf, J.K. (2021) *A Brief Introduction to Leadership*. Oslo: Universitetsforlaget.

Baer, M. & Frese, M. (2003) 'Innovation is not enough: Climates for initiative and psychological safety, process innovations, and firm performance.' *Journal of Organizational Behavior*, Vol. 24, No. 1, pp. 45–68.

Bang, H. & Midelfart, T.N. (2019) *Effektive ledergrupper [Effective Management Teams]*. Oslo: Gyldendal Akademisk.

Barnett, M., Jermier, J. & Lafferty, B. (2006) 'Corporate Reputation: The Definitional Landscape.' *Corporate Reputation Review*, Vol. 9, pp. 26–38.

Blyton, P. & Jenkins, J. (2007) *Key Concepts in Work*. London: Sage.

Bolman, L.G. & Deal, T.E. (2017) *Reframing Organizations. Artistry, Choice, and Leadership*, 6th edn. Hoboken: Wiley.

Bonvik, Ø. (2015) *Frist meg ikke inn i ledelse [Tempt Me Not into Leadership]*. Bergen: Fagbokforlaget.

Bonvik, Ø., Lorentz, C., & Martinsen, Ø. (2019) *På jobben [At Work]* [podcast], 16.09.2019.

Brandi, U. & Hasse, C. (2012) 'Employee-Driven Innovation and Practice-Based Learning in Organizational Cultures,' in Høyrup, S., Bonnafous-Boucher, M., Hasse, C., Lotz, M., & Møller, K. (eds) *Employee-Driven Innovation. A New Approach*. London: Palgrave Macmillan.

Breivik, M. & Larsen, V. (2020) *NRK Drivkraft [Drive]* [podcast], 10.08.2020.

Brenna, L.R. (2018) *Mangfoldsledelse. Mangfold og likestilling som bærekraftig konkurransefortrinn [Diversity Management. Diversity and Equality as a Sustainable Competitive Advantage]*. Oslo: Cappelen Damm.

Bringselius, L. (2021) *Tillitsbaserat ledarskap [Trust-Based Leadership]*. Helsingborg: Komlitt.

Brinkmann, S. (2019) *Brinkmanns Briks* [podcast], Dansk Radio, 20.03.2019.

Brønn, P.S. (2020) *Åpen eller innadvendt. Omdømmebygging for organisasjoner [Open or Introverted. Reputation Building for Organizations]*. Oslo: Gyldendal Akademisk.

Bungum, B., Forseth, U., & Kvande, E. (eds) (2015) *Den norske modellen. Internasjonalisering som utfordring og vitalisering [The Norwegian Model. Internationalization as a Challenge and Revitalization]*. Bergen: Fagbokforlaget.

Bupp, N. (1996) 'The Change Curve.' Paper presented at the High Performance Work Organization Partnership Seminar, Placid Harbor, 01.08.1996.

Bævre, A.I. (2019) 'Bli med på colonialmajor Reitans verdireise.' *Adresseavisen*, 25.03.2019.

Bøhn, E.D. (2019) *Meningen med livet [The Meaning of Life]*. Oslo: Spartacus.

Baas, M., De Dreu, C.K.W., & Nijstad, B.A. (2008) 'A meta-analysis of 25 years of mood-creativity research: Hedonic tone, activation, or regulatory focus?' *Psychological Bulletin*, Vol. 134, No. 6, pp. 779–806.

Cannella, A.A., Park, J.H., & Lee, H.U. (2008) 'Top Management Team Functional Background Diversity and Firm Performance: Examining the Roles of Team Member Colocation and Environmental Uncertainty.' *The Academy of Management Journal*, Vol. 51, No. 4, pp. 768–84.

Clampitt, P.G. (2013) *Communicating for Managerial Effectiveness. Problems, Strategies, Solutions*. Thousand Oaks: Sage.

Cohen-Charash, Y. & Spector, P.E. (2001) 'The Role of Justice in Organizations: A Meta-Analysis.' *Organizational Behavior and Human Decision Processes: A Journal of Fundamental Research and Theory in Applied Psychology*, Vol. 86, No. 2, pp. 278–321.

Conan Doyle, A. (1890/2014) *The Sign of Four*. London: Penguin.

Darsø, L. (2011) *Innovationspædagogik. Kunsten at fremelske innovationskompetence [Innovation Pedagogy. The Art of Promoting Innovation Competence]*. Copenhagen: Samfundslitteratur.

De Jong, J.P.J. & Kemp, R. (2003) 'Determinants of Co-Workers' Innovative Behaviour: An Investigation into Knowledge Intensive Services.' *International Journal of Innovation Management*, Vol. 7, No. 2, pp. 189–212.

Deci, E.L., Koestner, R., & Ryan, R.M. (1999) 'A meta-analytic review of experiments examining the effects of extrinsic rewards on intrinsic motivation.' *Psychological Bulletin*, Vol. 125, No. 6, pp. 627–68.

Deci, E.L. & Ryan, R.M. (1985) *Intrinsic Motivation and Self-Determination in Human Behavior*. New York: Plenum Press.

Delaney, L. & Lades, L. (2017) 'Present Bias and Everyday Self-Control Failures: A Day Reconstruction Study.' *Journal of Behavioral Decision Making*, Vol. 30, pp. 1157–67.

Edmondson, A. (2019) *The Fearless Organization. Creating Psychological Safety in the Workplace for Learning, Innovation and Growth*. Hoboken: Wiley.

Edmondson, A. (2023) *Right Kind of Wrong. Why Learning to Fail Can Teach Us to Thrive*. London: Penguin.

Eggen, N.A. (1999/2016) *Godfoten. Samhandling – veien til suksess [The Good Foot. Interaction — the Path to Success]*. Oslo: Aschehoug.

Eilertsen, T. & Glomnes, L. (2020) *Aftenpodden* [podcast], 13.08.2020.

Elrod, P.D. & Tippett, D.D. (2002) 'The Death Valley of Change.' *Journal of Organizational Change Management*, Vol. 15, No. 3, pp. 273–91.

Erwin, D.G. & Garman, A.N. (2010) 'Resistance to organizational change: linking research and practice.' *Leadership & Organization Development Journal*, Vol. 31, pp. 39–56.

Ettlie, J.E. (2006) *Managing Innovation. New Technology, New Products and New Services in a Global Economy*. Oxford: Butterworth-Heinemann.

Fackler, M. (2012) 'Critics say Japan ignored warnings of nuclear disaster.' *New York Times*, 10.02.2012.

Fikse, C. (2020) 'Relasjonell kapasitetsbygging for samskaping' [Relational capacity building for co-creation], in Myskja, A. & Fikse, C. (eds) *Perspektiver på livsmestring i skolen [Perspectives on Life Mastery in Schools]*. Oslo: Cappelen Damm Akademisk.

Fineman, S. (2000) 'Emotional Arenas Revisited,' in Fineman, S. (ed.) *Emotion in Organizations*. London: Sage.

Ford, J.D. & Ford, L.W. (2009) 'Decoding resistance to change: Strong leaders can hear and learn from their critics.' *Harvard Business Review*, Vol. 87, No. 4, pp. 99–103.

Foss, N.J. & Klein, P.G. (2022). *Why Managers Matter. The Perils of the Bossless Company*. New York: Hachette.

Foss, N.J., Minbaeva, D.B., Pedersen, T., & Reinholt, M. (2009) 'Encouraging knowledge sharing among employees: How job design matters.' *Human Resource Management*, Vol. 48, No. 6, pp. 871–83.

Fredrickson, B.L. (2001) 'The role of positive emotions in positive psychology: The broaden-and-build theory of positive emotions.' *American Psychologist*, Vol. 56, No. 3, pp. 218–26.

Frese, M. & Keith, N. (2015) 'Action Errors, Error Management, and Learning in Organizations.' *Annual Review of Psychology*, Vol. 66, No. 1, pp. 661–87.

Frey, B.S. & Jegen, R. (2001) 'Motivation crowding theory.' *Journal of Economic Surveys*, Vol. 15, No. 5, pp. 589–611.

Fyhn, B. (2023). 'Safe Today, Tomorrow, and Together: A Dynamic Perspective on Team Psychological Safety.' PhD dissertation, NHH Norwegian School of Economics.

Garborg, R. & Kjerpeseth, J.E. (2019) *Preik [Talk]* [podcast], 31.10.2019.

Geissler, H. (2018) *Seasonal Associate*. Los Angeles: Semiotext.

George, J.M. (2000) 'Emotions and Leadership: The Role of Emotional Intelligence.' *Human Relations*, Vol. 53, No. 8, pp. 1027–55.

Giertsen, T. & Giæver, A. (2020) *VG Giæver og gjengen [Giæver and the Gang]* [podcast], 20.03.2020.

Gjøsund, G. (2009) 'Medarbeidermedvirkning' [Participation], in Hepsø, I.L. & Kongsvik, T. (eds) *Forskning som endringsverktøy i organisasjoner. Forståelse, utvikling og praksis [Research as a Tool for Change in Organizations. Understanding, Development and Practice]*. Trondheim: Tapir akademisk forlag.

Glasø, L. & Martinsen, Ø.L. (2018) 'Forskning på selvledelse' [Research on self-management], in Glasø, L. & Thompson, G. (eds) *Selvledelse. Teori, forskning og praksis [Self-Management. Theory, Research and Practice]*. Oslo: Gyldendal Akademisk.

Glorvigen, M. (2019) 'Simon Sineks ideer' [The Ideas of Simon Sinek], *Aftenposten*, 21.06.19.

Graeber, D. (2018) *Bullshit Jobs. A Theory*. New York: Simon & Schuster.

Grann, I. (2019) 'Her skal man komme med originalemballasjen. En kvalitativ studie av hvordan læring utvikles i praksisfellesskap blant inkluderte deltagere i en dagligvarebutikk' [Here you must bring the original packaging. A qualitative study of how learning develops in a community of practice among included participants in a grocery store]. Master's thesis, Norwegian University of Science and Technology.

Gressgård, L.J., Amundsen, O., Aasen, T.M., & Hansen, K. (2014) 'Use of information and communication technology to support employee-driven innovation in organizations: A knowledge management perspective.' *Journal of Knowledge Management*, Vol. 18, No. 4, pp. 633–50.

Grimen, H. (2009) *Hva er tillit? [What Is Trust?]* Oslo: Universitetsforlaget.

Guddal, R. (2019) 'Jeg er stolt av å jobbe i NAV' [I am proud working at NAV], *VG*, 27.04.2019.

Halvorsen, K. & Apeland, O.C. (2020) *Lederliv [Life as a Leader]* [podcast], 07.01.2020.

Hamel, G. & Zanini, M. (2020) *Humanocracy. Creating Organizations as Amazing as the People Inside Them*. Boston: Harvard Business Review Press.

Hansen, K., Amundsen, O., Aasen, T.M., & Gressgård, L.J. (2017) 'Management Practices for Promoting Employee-Driven Innovation,' in Oeij, P.R.A., Rus, D., & Pot, F.D. (eds) *Workplace Innovation. Theory, Research and Practice*. Cham: Springer.

Harvey, F, Vidal, J., & Carrington, D. (2012) 'Dramatic fall in new nuclear power stations after Fukushima.' *The Guardian*, 08.03.2012.

Hemmestad, L.B. (2013) 'Balansekunst. Ledelse, læring og makt i håndballandslaget for kvinner senior' [Art of balance. Management, learning and power in the senior women's handball team]. PhD thesis, University of Southern Norway.

Hennestad, B.W. & Revang, Ø. (2017) *Endringsledelse og ledelsesendring — fra plan til praksis [Change Management and Management Change — from Plan to Practice]*. Oslo: Universitetsforlaget.

Hilland, J. & Kjerpeseth, J.E. (2019) *Preik [Talk]* [podcast], 07.10.2019.

Hofstad, K. & Rosvold, K.A. (2021) 'Fukushima — kjernekraftulykke' [Fukushima — nuclear accident]. Oslo: *SNL*.

Hollensbe, E., Wookeey, C., Hickey, L., & George, G. (2014) 'Organizations with purpose.' *Academy of Management Journal*, Vol. 57, No. 5, pp. 1227–34.

Hon, A.H.Y. (2012) 'Shaping environments conductive to creativity: The role of intrinsic motivation.' *Cornell Hospitality Quarterly*, Vol. 53, No. 1, pp. 53–64.

Horwitz, S.K. & Horwitz, I.B. (2007) 'The Effects of Team Diversity on Team Outcomes: A Meta-Analytic Review of Team Demography.' *Journal of Management*, Vol. 33, No. 6, pp. 987–1015.

Hülsheger, U.R., Anderson, N., & Salgado, J.F. (2009) 'Team-level predictors of innovation at work: A comprehensive meta-analysis spanning three decades of research.' *Journal of Applied Psychology*, Vol. 94, No. 5, pp. 1128–45.

Høgh-Olesen, H. (1995) 'Flertydighedsintolerance og stimulationssøgning: fortsatte studier af inertiens psykometri' [Ambiguity intolerance and stimulation seeking: continued studies of the psychometry of inertia], *Nordic Psychology*, Vol. 47, No. 1, pp. 14–28.

Høyrup, S. (2020) 'Medarbejderdreven innovation' [Employee-driven innovation], in Amble, N., Amundsen, O., & Rismark,

M. (eds) *Medarbeiderdrevet innovasjon [Employee-Driven Innovation]*. Oslo: Gyldendal Akademisk.

Høyrup, S., Bonnafous-Boucher, M., Hasse, C., Lotz, M., & Møller, K. (eds) (2012) *Employee-Driven Innovation. A New Approach*. London: Palgrave Macmillan.

Irgens, E.J. (2011) *Dynamiske og lærende organisasjoner. Ledelse og utvikling i et arbeidsliv i endring [Dynamic and Learning Organizations. Management and Development in a Changing Working Life]*. Bergen: Fagbokforlaget.

Isaacs, W. (1999) *Dialogue: The Art of Thinking Together*. New York: Random House.

Jacobsen, D.I. (2018) *Organizational Change and Change Management*. Bergen: Fagbokforlaget.

Jacobsen, D.I. & Thorsvik, J. (2019) *Hvordan organisasjoner fungerer [How Organizations Work]*. Bergen: Fagbokforlaget.

Jain, A., Dedieu, V., Zwetsloot, G., & Leka, S. (2017) 'Workplace Innovation and Wellbeing at Work: A Review of Evidence and Future Research Agenda,' in Oeij, P.R.A., Rus, D., & Pot, F.D. (eds) *Workplace Innovation. Theory, Research and Practice*. Cham: Springer.

Johansen, T., Specht, T., & Kleive, H. (2020) *Bæredygtig organisations og forretningsudvikling [Sustainable Organizational and Business Development]*. Copenhagen: Dansk psykologisk forlag.

Julsrud, T.E. (2018) *Organisatorisk tillit. Grunnlaget for samarbeid i nettverkenes tid [Organizational Trust. The Basis for Cooperation in the Age of Networks]*. Bergen: Fagbokforlaget.

Karlsen, J.E. (2015) 'For det felles beste,' in Karlsen, J.E. (ed.) *Veivisere i norsk organisasjonsforskning. Organisasjonsfaglig kanon [Guides in Norwegian Organizational Research. Organizational Canon]*. Bergen: Fagbokforlaget.

Karp, T. & Helgø, T.I. (2008) 'From Change Management to Change Leadership: Embracing Chaotic Change in Public Service Organizations.' *Journal of Change Management*, Vol. 8, No. 1, pp. 85–96.

Kaspersen, L. (2010) 'Lederens mål er ikke å få venner for livet.' [The leader's goal is not to make friends for life] *Dagens Næringsliv*, 23.09.2010.

Kaspersen, L. (2013) 'Y-faktoren som er bra både for deg og sjefen.' [Y-factor is good for you and the company] *Dagens Næringsliv*, 24.02.13.

Kaufmann, G. & Kaufmann, A. (2009/2015) *Psykologi i organisasjon og ledelse [Psychology in Organization and Management]*. Bergen: Fagbokforlaget.

Kellermann, B. (2004) *Bad Leadership. What It Is, How It Happens, Why It Matters*. Boston: Harvard Business School Press.

Klev, R. & Levin, M. (2012) *Participative Transformation. Learning and Development in Practising Change*. Burlington: Gower.

Klitmøller, A., Lauring, J., & Christensen, P.R. (2007) 'Medarbejderdreven innovation i den offentlige sektor' [Employee-driven innovation in the public sector]. *Ledelse & Erhvervsøkonomi*, Vol. 71, No. 4, pp. 207–16.

Knippenberg, D. & Sleebos, E. (2006) 'Organizational identification versus organizational commitment: Self-definition, social exchange, and job attitudes.' *Journal of Organizational Behavior*, Vol. 27, pp. 571–84.

Kongsvik, T.Ø. (2006) *Innviklet utvikling. En studie av en endringsprosess i Statoils anskaffelses og forsyningsvirksomhet [Complicated development. A study of a change process in Statoil's procurement and supply operations]*. Dr Polit. thesis, Norwegian University of Science and Technology.

Kuvaas, B. (ed.) (2008) *Lønnsomhet gjennom menneskelige ressurser. Evidensbasert HRM [Profitability through Human Resources. Evidence-Based HRM]*. Bergen: Fagbokforlaget.

Kuvaas, B. & Dysvik, A. (2020) *Lønnsomhet gjennom menneskelige ressurser. Evidensbasert HRM [Profitability through Human Resources. Evidence-Based HRM]*. Bergen: Fagbokforlaget.

Kvadsheim, S. (2021) 'En av fire vil skifte jobb.' *Finansavisen*, 28.05.2021.

Kvalnes, Ø. (2020) *Etikk og bærekraft [Ethics and Sustainability]*. Oslo: Universitetsforlaget.

Kværner, K. (2020) *Hjernemysterier [Brain Mysteries]*. Bergen: Fagbokforlaget.

Kvaal, I. (2014) 'Ekstrem oppussing på jobben.' [New look at work] *Dagens Nærligsliv*, 01.01.2014.

Le Coze, J.C. (2015). '1984–2014. Normal Accidents. Was Charles Perrow Right for the Wrong Reasons?' *Journal of Contingencies and Crisis Management*, Vol. 23, No. 4, pp. 275–86.

Lempiälä, T., Kauhaluoma, S.Y., & Näsänen, J. (2018) 'Similar structures, different interpretations: perceived possibilities for employee-driven innovation in two teams within an industrial organisation.' *International Journal of Entrepreneurship and Innovation Management*, Vol. 22, Nos 4–5, pp. 362–80.

Levin, M. & Klev, R. (2002) *Forandring som praksis. Læring og utvikling i organisasjoner [Change as Practice. Learning and Development in Organizations]*. Bergen: Fagbokforlaget.

Levin, M., Nilssen, T., Ravn, J.E., & Øyum, L. (2012) *Demokrati i arbeidslivet. Den norske samarbeidsmodellen som konkurransefortrinn [Democracy in Working Life. The Norwegian Cooperation Model as a Competitive Advantage]*. Bergen: Fagbokforlaget.

Lysklett, S.R. (2007) *Dialog mellom ideer: Ideutviklingens vilkår i arbeidsgruppemøter [Dialogue between ideas: The conditions for idea development in working group meetings*. Dr Art thesis, Norwegian University of Science and Technology.

Lyubomirsky, S., King, L., & Diener, E. (2005) 'The Benefits of Frequent Positive Affect: Does Happiness Lead to Success?' *Psychological Bulletin*, Vol. 131, No. 6, pp. 803–55.

Martin, A. (2021) 'Løsning av konflikter på arbeidsplassen ved hjelp av interessebaserte prosesser' [Resolving conflicts in the workplace using interest-based processes], in Klev, R. & Levin, M. (eds) *Forandring som praksis. Endring og utvikling som samskapt læring [Change as Practice. Change and Development as Co-Created Learning]*. Bergen: Fagbokforlaget.

Maslow, A.H. (1968) *Toward a Psychology of Being*. 2nd edn. Princeton: D. Van Nostrand.

Mayer, R.C., Davis, J.H., & Schoorman, D.F. (1995) 'An Integrative Model of Organizational Trust.' *The Academy of Management Review*, Vol. 20, No. 3, pp. 709–34.

McGregor, D. (1960) *The Human Side of Enterprise*. New York: McGraw-Hill.

McLean, L.D. (2005) 'Organizational Culture's Influence on Creativity and Innovation: A Review of the Literature and Implications for Human Resource Development.' *Advances in Developing Human Resources*, Vol. 7, No. 2, pp. 226–46.

Melsom, N. (2021) 'Fremtidens arbeidsliv' [The working life of the future], in Kongsvik, T., Moen, Ø., Vie, O.E., Jørgensen, R.B., & Albrechtsen, E. (eds) *Norsk arbeidsliv mot 2050. Muligheter og trusler [Nordic Working Life towards 2050. Opportunities and Threats]*. Bergen: Fagbokforlaget.

Meyer, C.B. & Stensaker, I.G. (2011) *Endringskapasitet [Change Capacity]*. Bergen: Fagbokforlaget.

Meyer, J.W. & Allen, N.J. (1997) *Commitment in the Workplace: Theory, Research and Application*. Thousand Oaks: Sage.

Michie, S.G., Dooley, R.S., & Fryxell, G.E. (2002) 'Top Management Team Heterogeneity, Consensus, and Collaboration: A Moderated Mediation Model of Decision Quality.' *Academy of Management Proceedings*, L1.

Milch, V. & Laumann, K. (2016) 'Interorganizational complexity and organizational accident risk: A literature review.' *Safety Science*, Vol. 82, pp. 9–17.

Moen, O.M. & Myrtveit, A.C. (2020) *NRK Verdibørsen* [podcast], 11.07.2020.

Moi, T. (2018) 'Om alternativer til toleranse.' [About alternative tolerance] *Morgenbladet*, 01.06.2018.

Muller, J.Z. (2018) *The Tyranny of Metrics*. Princeton: Princeton University Press.

Mustosmaki, A. (2017) *How Bright Are the Nordic Lights? Job Quality Trends in Nordic Countries in a Comparative Perspective*. Jyvaskyla: University of Jyvaskyla.

Newman, D.M. (1995) *Sociology. Exploring the Architecture of Everyday Life*. Thousand Oaks: Pine Forge Press.

Norvik, H. & Kjerpeseth, J.E. (2019) *Preik [Talk]* [podcast], 19.08.2019.

Norwegian University of Science and Technology (2023). *Knowledge for a Better World*. Trondheim: NTNU.

Nygårdsvik, I. (unpublished). *Integrert bedriftskommunikasjon* [*Integrated Company Communication*]. Bergen: Fagbokforlaget.

Nørmark, D. & Fogh Jensen, A. (2021) *Pseudowork: How We Ended Up Being Busy Doing Nothing*. Copenhagen: Gyldendal Trade.

Oddane, T. (2017) *Kreativitet og innovasjon. Fem sider av nesten samme sak [Creativity and Innovation. Five Sides of Almost the Same Issue]*. Bergen: Fagbokforlaget.

O'Donoghue, T. & Rabin, M. (1999) 'Doing It Now or Later.' *The American Economic Review*, Vol. 89, No. 1, pp. 103–24.

Olafsen, A.H. (2018) 'Selvbestemmelsesteorien: Et differensiert perspektiv på motivasjon i arbeidslivet' [The self-determination theory: A differentiated perspective on motivation in working life]. *Magma. Tidsskrift for økonomi og ledelse*, Vol. 18, No. 2, pp. 54–61.

Paradisi, M., Matera, C., & Nerini, A. (2024) 'Feeling Important, Feeling Well. The Association between Mattering and Well-Being: A Meta-Analysis Study.' *Journal of Happiness Studies*, Vol. 25, No. 4.

Parker, D. & Grandy, G. (2009) 'Looking to the past to understand the present: Organizational change in varsity sport.' *Qualitative Research in Organizations and Management: An International Journal*, Vol. 4, No. 3, pp. 231–54.

Payne, S.C. & Huffman, A.H. (2005) 'A longitudinal examination of the influence of mentoring on organizational commitment and turnover.' *Academy of Management Journal*, Vol. 48, pp. 158–68.

Pletten, C. (2021) 'Takk og farvel til jobben.' [Goodbye Work] *Aftenposten*, 11.06.2021.

Porter, L.W., Steers, R.M., Mowday, R.T., & Boulian, P.V. (1974) 'Organizational commitment, job satisfaction and turnover among psychiatric technicians.' *Journal of Applied Psychology*, Vol. 59, pp. 603–9.

Pot, F. (2017) 'Workplace Innovation and Wellbeing at Work,' in Oeij, P.R.A., Rus, D., & Pot, F.D. (eds) *Workplace Innovation. Theory, Research and Practice*. Cham: Springer.

Preuss, B. (2017). 'Nordic Management and Sustainable Business.' *Journal of Business and Financial Affairs*, Vol. 6, No. 2.

Prilleltensky, I. (2020). 'Mattering at the Intersection of Psychology, Philosophy, and Politics.' *American Journal of Community Psychology*, Vol. 65, pp. 16–34.

Rismark, M. & Amundsen, O. (2020) 'Omsorgsarbeidere i ekspansivt læringsmiljø' [Care workers in an expansive learning environment], in Amble, N., Amundsen, O., & Rismark, M. (eds) *Medarbeiderdrevet innovasjon [Employee-Driven Innovation]*. Oslo: Gyldendal Akademisk.

Ryan, R.M., & Deci, E.L. (2017) *Self-Determination Theory: Basic Psychological Needs in Motivation, Development, and Wellness*. New York: Guilford Press.

Rotenberg, K.J. (2018) *The Psychology of Trust*. London: Routledge.

Schiefloe, P.M. (2003) *Mennesker og samfunn. Innføring i sosiologisk forståelse [People and Society. Introduction to Sociological Understanding]*. Bergen: Fagbokforlaget.

Scott, C.D. & Jaffe, D.T. (2004) *Managing Change at Work. Leading People through Organizational Change*. Boston: Crisp Learning.

Seligman, M.E.P. & Schulman, P. (1986) 'Explanatory style as a predictor of productivity and quitting among life insurance sales agents.' *Journal of Personality and Social Psychology,* Vol. 50, No. 4, pp. 832–8.

Sergui, P.I., Șorcaru, S.L., Panaitescu, M., & Prunău, N.F. (2023) 'The low power distance in Nordic Management: an incentive for the regional learning by doing approach.' *Total Quality Management & Business Excellence* (19 June).

Sinek, S. (2009) *Start With Why: How Great Leaders Inspire Everyone to Take Action.* New York: Portfolio/Penguin.

Sinek, S. (2017) *Find Your Why: A Practical Guide for Discovering Purpose for You and Your Team.* New York: Portfolio/Penguin.

Sitkin, S.B. & Stickel, D. (1996) 'The Road to Hell. The Dynamics of Distrust in an Era of Quality,' in Kramer, R.M. & Tyler, T.R. (eds) *Trust in Organizations.* London: Sage.

Sjøvold, E. (2016) *Makt og maktbruk i arbeidslivet [Power and Use of Power in Working Life].* Oslo: Universitetsforlaget.

Skårderud, F. (2020) 'Nei, vi er ikke så gode til å lytte.' [We are bad listeners] *Aftenposten,* 14.08.2020.

Smith, P., Kesting, P., & Ulhøi, J.P. (2008) 'What are the driving forces of employee-driven innovation?' Paper presented at *9th International CINet Conference,* Valencia, Spain, 09.09.2008.

Spector, P.E. & Fox, S. (2010) 'Counterproductive Work Behavior and Organizational Citizenship Behavior: Are They Opposite Forms of Active Behavior?' *Applied Psychology: An International Review,* Vol. 59, No. 1, pp. 21–39.

Stensaker, I. & Haueng, A.C. (2016) *Omstilling. Den uforutsigbare gjennomføringsfasen [Change. The Unpredictable Implementation Phase].* Bergen: Fagbokforlaget.

Stensaker, I., Meyer, C.B., Falkenberg, J., & Haueng, A.C. (2001) 'Excessive Change: Unintended Consequences of Strategic Change.' Paper presented to the *Academy of Management Meetings,* Washington, DC.

Storeide, K. (2013) 'Lytting i lederskap. En kvalitativ intervjustudie av lederes opplevelse av lytting i utøvelse av lederskap' [Listening in leadership. A qualitative interview study of managers' experience of listening in the exercise of leadership]. Master's thesis in counseling, Norwegian University of Science and Technology.

Storey, J. & Salaman, G. (2005) *Managers of Innovation. Insights into Making Innovation Happen*. Oxford: Blackwell.

Storey, J. & Salaman, G. (2009) *Managerial Dilemmas: Exploiting Paradox for Strategic Leadership*. Chichester: Wiley.

Sund, B. (2019) *Typisk norsk å være (selv)god. En liten bok om den norske lederstilen [Typically Norwegian to Be Good. A Small Book about the Norwegian Leadership Style]*. Oslo: Cappelen Damm Akademisk.

Svendsen, L.F.H. (2015) *Work*. London: Routledge.

Svenningson, S. & Alvesson, M. (2016) *Managerial Lives. Leadership and Identity in an Imperfect World*. Cambridge: Cambridge University Press.

Sørhaug, T. (1996) *Om ledelse. Makt og tillit i moderne organisering [About Management. Power and Trust in Modern Organization]*. Oslo: Universitetsforlaget.

Tangen, N., Jones, M., & Sverdrup, T. (2021) *Ledertaffel* [podcast], 19.01.2021.

The New Oxford Dictionary of English (1989). London: Clarendon Press.

Thomas, D.A. & Ely, R.J. (1996) 'Making Differences Matter. A New Paradigm for Managing Diversity.' *Harvard Business Review*, Vol. 74, No. 5, pp. 79–90.

Thomas, R. & Hardy, C. (2011) 'Reframing resistance to organizational change.' *Scandinavian Journal of Management*, Vol. 27, pp. 322–31.

Thomas, W.I. & Thomas, D.S. (1928) *The Child in America: Behavior Problems and Programs*. New York: Knopf.

Tidd, J. & Bessant, J. (2009) *Managing Innovation. Integrating Technological, Market and Organizational Change*. London: Wiley.

Tjora, A. (2018) *Hva er fellesskap? [What Is Community?]*. Oslo: Universitetsforlaget.

Tomasgard, A. (2021) 'Globale transformasjoner utfordrer arbeidslivet' [Global transformations challenge working life], in Kongsvik, T., Moen, Ø., Vie, O.E., Jørgensen, R.B., & Albrechtsen, E. (eds) *Norsk arbeidsliv mot 2050. Muligheter og trusler [Norwegian Working Life towards 2050. Opportunities and Threats]*. Bergen: Fagbokforlaget.

Trulsen, O.N. (2011) 'Jobs var verdens verste sjef.' [Jobs was a bad boss] *NRK*, 24.10.2011.

Traaseth, A.K., Brenna, N., & Eia, H. (2020) *NRK Sånn er du [This Is You]* [podcast], 17.08.2020.

Van de Ven, A., Polley, D., Garud, R., & Venkataraman, S. (1999) *The Innovation Journey*. New York: Oxford University Press.

Van Scotter, J.R. & Motowidlo, S.J. (1996) 'Interpersonal Facilitation and Job Dedication as Separate Facets of Contextual Performance.' *Journal of Applied Psychology*, Vol. 81, No. 5, pp. 525–31.

Vanebo, J.O. (2016) *Ledelse og ledelsespraksis i det offentlige. Veikart til ledelseslisens [Management and Management Practice in the Public Sector. Roadmap to Management Licence]*. Oslo: Universitetsforlaget.

Vestergaard, B. (2012) 'Leading Unpopular Changes with Fair Proces: Towards a Strategic Process Design.' *Academy of Management Annual Meeting Proceedings*, Vol. 2012, No. 1.

Vie, O.E. (2012) 'Ledelse på norsk' [Management in Norwegian]. *Magma. Tidsskrift for økonomi og ledelse*, Vol. 16, No. 2, pp. 60–7.

Von Oettingen, A. & Mellon, K. (eds) (2020) *Pissedårlig ledelse [Piss-Poor Leadership]*. Copenhagen: Hans Reitzels Forlag.

Wilhelmsen, P.N. (2018) 'Drømmer du om å klaske knyttneven i pulten til sjefen og fortelle at du ikke kan sparkes fordi du slutter?' [Do you dream about quitting?] *Nettavisen*, 20.06.2018.

Wilkinson, A., Gollan, P.J., Marchington, M., & Lewin, D. (2010) 'Conceptualizing Employee Participation in Organizations,' in Wilkinson, A., Gollan, P.J., Marchington, M., & Lewin, D.

(eds) *The Oxford Handbook of Participation in Organizations*. New York: Oxford University Press.

Wilkinson, A., Gollan, P.J., Marchington, M., & Lewin, D. (eds) (2010) *The Oxford Handbook of Participation in Organizations*. New York: Oxford University Press.

Woodward, S. & Hendry, C. (2004) 'Leading and coping with change.' *Journal of Change Management*, Vol. 4, No. 2, pp. 155–83.

Ørsted, C. (2020) *Fatale forandringer. Forstå forandringsledelse i en uforudsigelig verden [Lethal Changes. Understanding Change Management in an Unpredictable World]*. Copenhagen: People's Press.

Aagestad, C., Tynes, T., Sterud, T., Johannessen, H.A., Gravseth, H.M., Løvseth, E.K., Alfonso, J.H., & Aasnæss, S. (2015) *Faktabok om arbeidsmiljø og helse 2015. Status og utviklingstrekk [Fact Book on Working Environment and Health 2015. Status and Trends]. STAMI-rapport 2015: 3*. Oslo: Statens arbeidsmiljøinstitutt.

Aasen, T.M. & Amundsen, O. (2011) *Innovasjon som kollektiv prestasjon [Innovation as a Collective Achievement]*. Oslo: Gyldendal Akademisk.

Aasen, T.M. & Amundsen, O. (2015) *Innovasjonsarbeid. Organisasjon, kultur og ledelse [Innovation Work. Organization, Culture and Management]*. Oslo: Gyldendal Akademisk.

Aasen, T.M., Amundsen, O., Gressgård, L.J., & Hansen, K. (2012) 'In search of best practices for employee driven innovation: Experiences from Norwegian work life,' in Høyrup, S., Bonnafous-Boucher, M., Hasse, C., Lotz, M., & Møller, K. (eds) *Employee-Driven Innovation. A New Approach*. London: Palgrave Macmillan.

Business Books

Business Books publishes practical guides and insightful non-fiction for beginners and professionals. Covering aspects from management skills, leadership and organizational change to positive work environments, career coaching and self-care for managers, our books are a valuable addition to those working in the world of business.

Recent bestsellers from Business Books are:

From 50 to 500

Jonathan Dapra, Richard Dapra and Jonas Akerman

An engaging and innovative small business leadership framework guaranteed to strengthen a leader's effectiveness to drive company growth and results.

Paperback: 978-1-78904-743-1 ebook: 978-1-78904-744-8

Be Visionary

Marty Strong

Be Visionary: Strategic Leadership in the Age of Optimization

Demonstrates to existing and aspiring leaders the positive impact of applying visionary creativity and decisiveness to achieve spectacular long-range results while balancing the day-to-day.

Paperback: 978-1-78535-432-8 ebook: 978-1-78535-433-5

Finding Sustainability

Trent A. Romer

Journey to eight states, three national parks and three countries to experience the life-changing education that led Trent A. Romer to find sustainability for his plastic-bag manufacturing business and himself.

Paperback: 978-1-78904-601-4 ebook: 978-1-78904-602-1

Inner Brilliance, Outer Shine

Estelle Read

Optimise your success, performance, productivity and well-being to lead your best business life.

Paperback: 978-1-78904-803-2 ebook: 978-1-78904-804-9

Tomorrow's Jobs Today
Rafael Moscatel and Abby Jane Moscatel
Discover leadership secrets and technology strategies being pioneered by today's most innovative business executives and renowned brands across the globe.
Paperback: 978-1-78904-561-1 ebook: 978-1-78904-562-8

Secrets to Successful Property Investment
Deb Durbin
Your complete guide to building a property portfolio.
Paperback: 978-1-78904-818-6 ebook: 978-1-78904-819-3

The Effective Presenter
Ryan Warriner
The playbook to professional presentation success!
Paperback: 978-1-78904-795-0 ebook: 978-1-78904-796-7

The Beginner's Guide to Managing
Mikil Taylor
A how-to guide for first-time managers adjusting to their new leadership roles.
Paperback: 978-1-78904-583-3 ebook: 978-1-78904-584-0

Forward
Elizabeth Moran
A practical playbook for leaders to guide their teams through their organization's next big change.
Paperback: 978-1-78279-289-5 ebook: 978-1-78279-291-8

Readers of ebooks can buy or view any of these bestsellers by clicking on the live link in the title. Most titles are published in paperback and as an ebook. Paperbacks are available in traditional bookshops. Both print and ebook formats are available online.

Find more titles and sign up to our readers' newsletter at www.collectiveinkbooks.com/fiction

PGIL2024USA